Switch
The
Algorithm

BN Publications LLC
PO BOX 60194
Nashville, TN 37206

Copyright @ 2024 by Laquawnteiss Clark
All rights reserved.

All rights reserved. No part of this book may be reproduced or transmitted in any form or by means, electronic or mechanical, including photocopying, recording, or by any information storage and retrieval system, without written permission from publisher.

While some incidents in this book are true, the names and personal characteristics of those described may have been changed to protect their privacy. Any resemblance to persons living or dead is entirely incidental and unintentional.

Names: Laquawnteiss "Coach Q" Clark, 1980 August 18-Author
Title: Switch the Algorithm / Laquawnteiss Clark.

Book cover Design: by Tariq Khan
Cover Photo: Jodie Smith
Photo credit: Page 154

Manufactured in the United States of America
Published in Nashville, TN by BN Publications LLC
ISBN: 979-8-218-53656-5
10 9 8 7 6 5 4 3 2

To my children, who are my driving force,
my greatest teachers, and my endless inspiration.
To my parents, whose unwavering love has shown me the true
meaning of unconditional support.
To my grandmother, who instilled in me the understanding
that family is the foundation of all that truly matters.
And to my readers may these pages awaken the greatness within
you and inspire you to pursue it relentlessly.

With all my love,
Coach Q

Preface 7

ONE | Since Covid 10

TWO | Pivotal Thoughts 23

THREE | Too Many Followers 39

FOUR | 50/50 53

FIVE | Girl Dad/MANnerisms 64

SIX | HoodGeek 75

SEVEN | The Goal is the Goal 90

EIGHT | It's a Trend 101

NINE | Designer Habits 110

TEN | Bring the love back 120

CONCLUSION | A Call to Switch the Algorithm 129

Poem | New Balance by Raegan Paige 137

Song Lyrics 139

Acknowledgements 164

About the Author 165

Preface

It feels somewhat surreal to be publishing my first ever book at what seems like such a strange time. We're living in a time where everyone seems to be on a healing journey, navigating confusion, misinformation, and the constant search for something that truly feels fulfilling. We are living in a world where discipline and commitment are nothing more than hashtags.

The world has become completely saturated with noise, pulling us in a thousand different directions. We're overstimulated and overwhelmed, and with this we're seeing a surge in mental health issues. Therapy is more sought after than ever before, but even as we seek healing, we're surrounded by triggers that make it hard to find peace. We've become reactive, constantly on edge, struggling to find our footing in a world that's moving too fast.

It is important to understand that our life is dictated by patterns; algorithms that control our every thought. These algorithms are the unseen forces that dictate what we see, how we think, and the choices we make. But those algorithms aren't just lines of code in social media platforms; they are the habits, thoughts, and mindsets that define how we move through life. We follow these patterns, often without question, allowing them to shape who we are, how we feel, and what we believe is possible.

But what if we could change them? What if we could switch the algorithm?

This book, Switch the Algorithm, was born out of a deep need to address these challenges proactively. It's not just about coping; it's about reclaiming control. It's about guarding the door to your mind, standing watch over what you allow in, and making intentional choices that lead to a life of purpose and direction. We need to shift from being pulled by the currents of society to creating motion with intent moving with purpose, not just for the sake of moving.

I remember listening to "Victory Lap" by Nipsey Hustle repeatedly during some of the toughest months of my life. The saying 'The marathon continues', seemingly passed away with Nipsey and we have become obsessed with the sprint.

Switch the Algorithm isn't just a book; it's a blueprint, a guide, and a call to action. It's about taking back control of your mind, your time, and your life. It's about getting back to the basics of discipline and commitment, creating motion with clear direction and purpose. It's about finding fulfillment in the things that truly matter your values, your growth, your relationships.

In addition to this book, I created an album where each chapter has an accompanying song that serves as my musical standpoint on the subject. This album is more than just a soundtrack; it's essentially an audiobook in music form. The songs capture the essence of each chapter, bringing the themes to life in a way that only music can. The book and album complement each other, combining words and music to motivate, challenge, and uplift.

Within these pages, I share my thoughts on the complexities of Black relationships, the struggle to find purpose, and the risks of living in an overstimulated world. But more than that, you'll find actionable advice, practical strategies, and the mindset shifts that can help you navigate these challenges and come out stronger on the other side.

As you read through these chapters and listen to the accompanying songs, I hope you'll find the inspiration, the tools, and the motivation to switch your own algorithm. To create a life that's not just about survival, but about thriving—living with purpose, direction, and fulfillment. Because at the end of the day, it's not about how fast you're moving or how much you're chasing—it's about what you're moving towards and why.

Let's switch the algorithm, together.

CHAPTER ONE

Since Covid

"The world changed overnight, forcing us to confront who we are when everything stops, and the distractions fade away."

My grandmother and I shared a Sunday tradition, watching football and listening to her vent about how the Tennessee Titans "are not about to do nothing". January 26, 2020, marked a day that would change everything. I remember going to her house this Sunday to watch the pro bowl and the most unexpected news break came across the screen. The news broke that Kobe Bryant, and his daughter Gianna had tragically passed away in a helicopter crash. In that moment, it felt like time stood still. My grandmother and I sat there, trying to comprehend how someone like Kobe, a figure who seemed almost invincible, could be gone. It wasn't just the shock; it felt like the world was giving us a sign. From that day on, life started to shift in ways I couldn't explain. As the months went by, the world around us seemed to turn upside down, as if everything had been reset, and nothing felt the same again.

Soon after, we launched Pivot Technology School's first class at the Lab on Jefferson Street. It felt like the start of something powerful, a real beginning. What I soon discovered was that life had a plan of its own. On March 3, 2020, a tornado ripped through Nashville, tearing the roof off the very building where we were supposed to kick off our vision. COVID-19 followed behind and as we were trying to rebuild, the entire world shut down. Everything we thought was solid suddenly became uncertain overnight. What followed was a whirlwind and suddenly, life shifted into an unrecognizable new reality, forcing me and so many others to rethink how we would navigate forward.

"Since Covid, it's hard to comprehend it / We lost connection, we obsessed with all of the pretending."

Life started to feel like as if it were unraveling and we were losing touch; not just with each other, but with who we really are. Everyone was trying to hold it together, putting on a brave face, but underneath, we were all struggling with this new reality. I thought to myself, *If there's ever been a time to put everything into building Pivot, it's now.* With life slowing down, it seemed like the perfect moment to lock in and bring that vision to life. But that calm focus didn't last as questions started piling up: How serious was Covid? Should we get vaccinated? And then, my grandmother, my anchor, caught the virus and had to be placed in rehab. One of the hardest moments was being unable to visit her in person, as Covid concerns had restricted access to the facility. The family was forced to stand outside her window, separated by glass, trying to connect however we could. It was a relentless storm of family, business, and survival, with everything feeling like it was teetering on the edge.

That time showed me just how important structure and focus really are. What seemed like the perfect opportunity to build something turned into a reminder that even with all the time in the world, without the right foundation, everything can feel like it's falling apart. The real question isn't whether you have time but whether you have focus. *Where is your focus?*

Before the pandemic, so many of us believed that if the world just slowed down, we would finally have the time to do the things we said were holding us back. We told ourselves we were too busy, that our dreams were on hold because of external circumstances. Then the pandemic struck, and in an instant, the world came to a standstill. We had all the time we could ever ask for, yet we still found ourselves struggling. Why? Because time was never the real issue. It was *purpose.*

"Frustration overload got us lacking decency / Everything is right there if you could match the frequency."

These lyrics reflect the overstimulation epidemic that surged after the lockdowns. With the world paused and nowhere to go, millions of us turned to our phones seeking comfort, distraction, and entertainment in a time of isolation. Social media quickly became the new reality, a virtual lifeline to a world we could no longer access in person. We became obsessed with the idea that we could transform ourselves in an instant, convinced that a 60-second Instagram reel or a quick TikTok video held the secret to cracking the code of self-improvement. Everywhere we turned, people were selling the illusion that, by the end of this pandemic, we could emerge as an entirely new version of ourselves—better, faster, more efficient.

But the truth is, we bought into a lie. What we were really chasing was attention, because in this new digital economy, attention became the ultimate currency. We all sought the quickest path to validation, the fastest route to recognition, believing that the more we consumed or produced, the more fulfilled we'd become. But the reality hit hard that this constant bombardment of content didn't heal or nourish us. Instead, it exposed the emptiness beneath the surface, deepening the void we were trying to fill. We were drowning in information, yet none of it provided the sustenance we truly needed. What we consumed was instant gratification at best, and at worst, a never-ending cycle of noise that left us more disconnected from our true selves.

Covid exposed something deeper: we didn't know what we really wanted.

Many of us had been living on autopilot, going through the motions, using our busy lives as excuses for not pursuing our real dreams. But when the noise of everyday life stopped, we were left to face ourselves and a lot of us didn't like what we saw. We realized that the problem wasn't time; it was the lack of direction, the absence of a clear purpose guiding our actions. And that realization hit hard.

The Epidemic of Overstimulation

During the pandemic, social media didn't just become a distraction, it became an addiction. People were constantly consuming content, comparing their lives to what they saw online, and falling into the trap of thinking that success could be instant. Millionaires popped up overnight, selling dreams of quick wealth and shortcuts to success. But here's the truth: *those shortcuts lead to dead ends*. People bought into the lie that if they just followed a few simple steps, they could have everything they wanted. But when the quick fixes didn't deliver, frustration set in, and the cycle of comparison and self-doubt intensified.

This overstimulation didn't just affect our goals; it affected our mental health. Social media, once a place of connection, became a breeding ground for insecurity. We were all scrolling through curated images of success and happiness, wondering why we didn't measure up. And when the reality of our lives didn't match the highlight reels we saw online, it made us feel even more isolated, more anxious, more disconnected.

"Depression like an obsession, but at least he bought him a Benz"

We've mastered the art of curating online personas, making it look like we have everything together, while inside, many of us are quietly struggling. We're stuck in this cycle of pretending, projecting perfection when we're only widening the gap between who we are and who we think we *should* be. It's like we're all running on a treadmill, trying to keep up with this impossible standard that leaves us feeling disconnected, frustrated, and, at times, lost. This constant striving to look the part is draining us daily and the truth is, it's pulling us further from the authenticity we need to really thrive.

In my view, the pandemic did more than just expose the flaws in our systems; it held up a mirror to the cracks in our own identities. So many of us had built our sense of self on external markers; what others thought of us, what we achieved, what we owned. When everything slowed down, those things lost their grip, and we were left with only ourselves, forced to confront the emptiness we'd been too busy to notice before. From my perspective, this moment stripped away the noise, leaving us face-to-face with what we had been avoiding.

The Obsession with Pretending

Since Covid, one of the most damaging shifts has been how we've leaned into these curated realities online, crafting lives that look perfect while hiding what's really happening beneath the surface. Before the pandemic, social media was already a place to showcase the highlight reel, but when our physical worlds suddenly shrank, the digital one became a kind of escape. We began living more through the filtered lens of what we wanted others to see, even as we struggled in private. Behind every "perfect" post, people were coping with fear, uncertainty, and isolation. Yet, somehow, we became even more skilled at pretending, projecting stability and success when so many of us were feeling anything but. The disconnect between our lives and our screens grew, and we've found ourselves playing along, hiding behind these carefully built facades instead of dealing with what's real.

I'll never forget the moment when I was in the thick of building my brand online, all while navigating the emotional strain of a divorce. It felt like I was living two separate lives at once. One on display for the world, showcasing a vision of success and self-assurance, while the other was privately unraveling, full of doubt, grief, and the weight of change. There was a critical point in that journey where everything became clear: I had to stop trying to circumvent the process. There was no shortcut through the pain, no way to bypass the personal journey that had to happen.

It was then that I realized something essential, we all face similar fears, pressures, and life-altering moments. We tend to isolate ourselves in these struggles, thinking we're the only ones who are broken or stuck, but the human experience is one of constant growth, loss, and rebirth. The real shift in my mindset came when I stopped resisting what was happening and started fully embracing it. I stopped running from the discomfort, and instead, I focused on owning everything including the pain, the mistakes, and the fears that came with this pivotal moment in my life.

What I discovered was that we aren't fixed. We aren't bound to who we were or where we came from. We have the power to evolve, to break free from patterns that no longer serve us, and to redefine what's possible for our future. It was this realization that became my power. The fastest route to growth, to a new future, wasn't through avoiding discomfort, but through real accountability.

We're sold this illusion that we're just one step away, almost there. But the truth is, this chase for manufactured perfection is wearing us down. It's like trying to grab smoke and no matter how close we get, it's always slipping just out of reach. Every day, we're hit with these images of "success," "happiness," and "luxury," each one making us question if we're enough or if we're falling behind. This constant barrage creates a subtle but constant anxiety and frustration that leaves us feeling trapped in a loop.

It's surreal how quickly titles have turned into the new standard for self-worth. Since the pandemic, it's like everyone suddenly wanted to be a CEO or boss, wearing these labels as if they alone could transform lives overnight. I've seen people jump into entrepreneurship, convinced by social media's promise that true success lies in self-employment and luxury. But much of what gets shown online creates an illusion rather than a foundation. What's missing is the stories of sacrificed families and missed payroll cycles. The reality that 90% of new businesses fail in the first year are left out of the story. And here's the issue: when we start chasing status over substance, we're left holding empty titles. True impact comes from the focus, the vision, and the work that goes on when the cameras aren't rolling.

I've had countless conversations with people claiming they were "grinding" to build an empire, but the reality was different once you dug a little deeper. Their focus was on looking the part, not putting in the real work it takes to truly be the part. There's nothing wrong with wanting to be a boss, to achieve greatness, but wearing the title isn't the same as carrying the weight of what that title requires. The pandemic had a lot of people rushing to embody a lifestyle that wasn't sustainable because it was rooted in appearance, not substance.

If I am being fully transparent, I am not immune to these pressures. I've felt that weight, the urge to show the world I've got it all together. When you're surrounded by messages telling you that you're only as good as what you achieve, it's easy to fall into the performance trap. But here's the truth I had to learn navigating rapping, corporate life and now entrepreneurship, it has to be in you, not on you. Real success? It's not about appearances. It's about building a foundation from within.

Self-work is the foundation where everything begins and where real change happens. You've got to be willing to dig deep, face your own insecurities, and sit with the discomfort that maybe, just maybe, you've been chasing things that will never truly satisfy you. For me, that meant pulling back from the noise, tuning out what everyone else was doing, and having an honest conversation with myself: Was I building something meaningful, something that resonated with my purpose, or was I caught up in maintaining a façade image.

The reality is we cannot skip this process. You must do the inner work to find your own peace, your own grounding, and your own direction. Without it, the pressure will always be there, pulling you into someone else's narrative. The only way to escape this cycle of comparison and pretension is to dive into the parts of yourself that need healing and take control of your own story. Until we stop pretending, we can't start healing. We can't begin to build something real if we're more focused on how it looks than how it feels.

So, ask yourself: Are you building something genuine, or are you caught up in the chase for appearances? The real work isn't easy, but it's the only path to the peace and fulfillment we're all after. Deep down, the answers are there, waiting for you to tap in.

The Rise of Therapy and Quick Fixes

Lately it seems challenging to come across someone that is not in therapy. Since Covid, I've seen more people opening about the need to take care of their minds and spirits. But if I'm being honest, I think there's a disconnect for a lot of people between saying they're in therapy and committing to the work it takes to grow.

It's easy to scroll past a quick motivational reel or watch a self-help video and feel a spark of inspiration, but from my experience, that spark fades fast. Real growth, the kind that sticks, takes more than surface-level solutions. We're used to the quick hit, but for lasting change, you must go way below the surface, and that can't happen in 60 seconds. In my own journey, I've found that true change requires being consistent, being patient, and pushing past that need for instant results. That's where the real progress is.

"Recently, seem like the therapist making all the bread; Cause a couple of tik tok reels can't help you get ahead."

Therapy has its place, but from my perspective, real change takes time and a lot of hard work. You can't expect to watch a few motivational clips, read a self-help book, and think you're done. It goes so much deeper than that. Real growth means confronting your pain, understanding your patterns, and putting in the time to rewire the way you think and operate.

The allure of shortcuts is powerful, and in today's world, it's tempting to take the easy route. Whether it's using Ozempic to lose weight without breaking a sweat or opting for surgery to achieve an "instant" transformation, we're surrounded by options that promise quick fixes. We live in an era where it's easier than ever to bypass the hard work, the struggle, and the process that not only shape our bodies but also develop our character.

Now, I'm not against the tools that help us get where we want to be. There's a time and place for interventions and sometimes they're essential, even life changing. And, in some cases, they can serve as vital support when used in the right way. But here's the deeper issue: when shortcuts become the norm, when we start relying on them as a substitute for the sweat, the grind, and the sacrifice, we rob ourselves of the growth that comes from the process itself. True strength, whether physical, mental, or emotional does not come from what we avoid, but from what we overcome. Without the work, we lose the resilience, the patience, and the sense of accomplishment that make us who we are. And in the long run, what we gain quickly can be lost just as fast.

We're in this culture where everything promises to be fast and easy, where you can change yourself without ever having to confront who you are. It's the same with "hustle culture" hacks, where success is painted as something you can "hack" rather than build. But when we skip the process, we're denying ourselves the real transformation, the growth that only comes from investing in the journey itself.

The creation phase is actually where the fulfillment lives. Without it, the victory feels hollow because we haven't given ourselves the chance to evolve. You can lose the weight, achieve the look, or land the title, but without the work, without the journey, it's just surface-level. Real fulfillment is about who you become as you move toward the goal, the grit you build when you push through, and the confidence that comes when you realize you've earned it.

The Dark Cloud of Depression

Covid didn't just expose the cracks in our systems; it exposed the cracks in our mental health. Depression and anxiety rates skyrocketed during the pandemic, and it's not hard to understand why. When you're constantly bombarded with images of other people's success and happiness, it's easy to feel like you're falling behind.

We've reached a point where it's easier to buy distractions than confront the real issues. People are hurting, but they're still posting, still flexing, still maintaining the illusion that everything's fine. It's like we've mastered the art of looking successful, but internally, we're struggling. And until we're ready to stop pretending and start confronting the truth, we'll stay stuck in this cycle.

A New Normal, A New Opportunity

The Covid era pulled back the curtain on how lost we can become without clear direction. We don't need more time; we need intention. Since then, it's like we've been bombarded with misinformation and quick-fix solutions from every angle, feeding a culture of confusion and division. And look, Trump didn't create this weaponized misinformation game, but he amplified it, turning confusion into a tactic. Now everyone—from influencers to brands to politicians—has picked up the playbook, keeping us searching, disoriented, and, most importantly, divided.

They've learned that as long as we're chasing the next quick fix or caught up in the latest "crisis" without real solutions, we stay distracted from what really matters. But the truth is, if we can tune out the noise, we can create something far deeper, something rooted in focus and discipline. There's a chance now to build a life that aligns with our true values, but we have to reject the easy outs and the empty noise that tell us to look outside ourselves for purpose.

We've seen how quickly the world can change, how fast everything can fall apart. But we've also seen that even when everything stops, we still have the power to create, to build, and to thrive. We can choose to rise above the noise, or we can stay stuck in the illusions that have kept us distracted for so long. *The choice is ours.*

"Since Covid, it done got dark / Damn baby, where do I start."

Things have gotten dark, no doubt, but we have the power to bring the light back. It starts with being honest about where we are, about what we're feeling, and about the work we need to do to heal. The post-Covid world can be the catalyst for something better, but it requires focus, discipline, and a commitment to real growth.

How You Can Change Your Algorithm:

1. Start with Honesty

Take a hard look at where you are. Are you living in alignment with your values? Are you hiding behind distractions or pretending everything's fine when it's not? True change begins with honesty.

2. Focus on What Matters

Once you've identified what's not working, focus on what does. What are your core values? What's your purpose? Align your actions with those things and let go of the rest.

3. Embrace the Process

Real growth doesn't happen overnight. Be patient with yourself. Success isn't about quick wins; it's about showing up every day, doing the work, and trusting that the process will lead you where you need to be.

CHAPTER TWO

Pivotal Thoughts

"The way we think in key moments defines our future. It's time to break free from limiting beliefs and see beyond our present reality."

The way you think doesn't just influence your present; it shapes your future. "Pivotal Thoughts" is about embracing this power, pushing the boundaries of what you believe is possible, and cultivating a mindset that can transform your life. This chapter isn't just a reflection on ideas, it's a challenge to you, to think bigger, go deeper, and use your thoughts to create the future you desire.

Every moment of our waking life, we make decisions. Some are small, almost trivial, but others have the power to completely change our lives. In 2009, I made one of those pivotal decisions when I chose to stop rapping. I had a full 17-song album, ready to release, but something inside me said I was meant for more. At that point, I had two sons and a 2-year-old daughter, and I knew I had untapped potential beyond music. So, I decided to go back to school and pursue Data Analytics, a choice that would change the direction of my entire life.

People around me couldn't understand why I would stop something they associated with my identity. They couldn't see the future I envisioned for myself because God hadn't given them that vision. He gave it to me. Often, people can only understand your path after it unfolds. Despite external pressure, I thought beyond my present and embraced something bigger. That shift led to growth in tech leadership, co-founding HoodGeek, Focal Point Solutions, and eventually Pivot Tech School. None of it would've been possible without those pivotal thoughts and the belief that something unseen was waiting to unfold.

Why Your Mindset Matters

Your mindset is the foundation of everything you do. It's the lens through which you view the world, and it determines how you respond to the challenges and opportunities that life presents. Too often, we allow our thoughts to be shaped by external influences without realizing the impact this has on our lives. But the truth is, the thoughts you entertain can either push you forward or hold you back.

Think about it: How many times have you been excited to pursue something, only to hear that voice in your head whispering, "What if it doesn't work out?" Or even worse, "What if you're not good enough?" I've been there feeling the weight of those thoughts, questioning if I could pull off something big, like building Pivot or starting my own business. These aren't just fleeting doubts; they're pivotal thoughts—moments where your entire path can shift based on what you choose to believe. In those moments, you can either lean into the fear and let it hold you back, or you can choose courage, act, and see what happens. That choice is what shapes the course of your life.

"I'm a student of excellence… borderline perfectionist, conversational specialist… the one that they are investing with."

Excellence isn't about never making mistakes or being perfect. Excellence is consistently striving to improve, pushing beyond what you think is possible, and refining your skills to create something of value. It's about taking deliberate action and being intentional in everything you do, whether in your personal relationships, your career, or your creative pursuits.

This concept of excellence became something I call "I didn't say it would be perfect, I just said I wasn't going to stop." It's not about perfection, but persistence. This approach has shaped how I move through life whether I'm launching a business, mastering a new skill, or striving to be a better partner or parent. The pursuit of excellence isn't about never making mistakes or having everything figured out from the start. It's about committing to the process, knowing that setbacks will come, and refusing to give up when they do.

This mindset is pivotal in everything we do. Your thoughts will either fuel you to push through those tough moments or hold you back, keeping you stuck in doubt and hesitation. I've had plenty of moments when I wasn't sure if things would work out, but I kept reminding myself—this isn't about getting it perfect the first time. It's about not stopping, not folding when things get hard, and staying committed to the vision. That's the essence of excellence: knowing the journey will have its ups and downs but deciding that no matter what, you won't stop moving forward.

Too often, we hesitate because of fear or the false belief that we're not ready. But if you're waiting for the perfect moment or for the stars to align before you act, you'll be waiting forever. Excellence is found in the doing, in the learning, in the iterative process of growth. That's why your mindset matters it's the difference between dreaming and doing.

The Power of Subconscious Programming

Your subconscious mind is powerful. It's where your deepest beliefs, fears, and programming reside, and these thoughts silently guide your actions in ways you might not even realize. Many of the decisions you make every day are automatic responses triggered by subconscious programming that has been built over time. They are preprogrammed from childhood, from societal expectations, and from the experiences you've had along the way.

Think about the time you wanted to make a bold move like switching careers, starting that business you've been dreaming about, or getting serious about your health. Most of us have faced that pivotal moment when we were ready to make a change, only to hear that voice in the back of our minds whisper, "Are you sure you can do this?"

Where did that doubt come from? It's likely the result of years of subconscious programming telling you to play it safe, to not rock the boat. Maybe you wanted to quit your 9-5 and start something of your own but talked yourself out of it. Or maybe you thought about enrolling in school, learning a new skill, or even taking a personal risk like stepping into a serious relationship, only to convince yourself it wasn't the right time. The fear of stepping too far outside of your comfort zone often stems from experiences and ideas that we've unknowingly internalized over time.

Your subconscious is constantly at work, shaping how you see the world. The key is to become aware of how your thoughts and beliefs are influencing your actions. Once you identify those limiting beliefs, you can start to challenge them. You can begin to reprogram your mind, replacing those automatic, limiting responses with thoughts that empower you to take risks, to grow, and to embrace new opportunities.

This realization is what led me to become Coach Q and get completely obsessed with understanding how and where real change happens. I wanted to know why some people, despite all odds, rise to the top, while others with seemingly endless potential stay stuck in the same patterns. It wasn't enough for me to just change my own life; I needed to understand the mechanics of transformation so I could help others do the same.

They say we change for one of two reasons: inspiration or desperation. For a lot of us, it's desperation that drives us to make that first move. We hit a point where the pain of staying the same outweighs the fear of change, and suddenly, we're forced to make a shift. But here's the thing, whether you're fueled by inspiration or desperation, the power to reprogram your mind and life is within you. Real change doesn't happen through sheer willpower alone; it happens when you take control of your subconscious mind and shift the beliefs that are holding you back.

That's why I became obsessed with this process. I wanted to dig into the root causes of our actions, to understand how those early years of programming shape the way we live, and how we can break free from the narratives that keep us limited. Once you start working on the inside, everything on the outside begins to change. The real magic happens when you realize that the power to change your entire life has always been within you.

Taking Responsibility for Your Own Growth

One of the most liberating and challenging truths is that you are responsible for your own growth. It's easy to blame external factors like your upbringing, your job, the people around you for why things aren't going the way you want. But real change happens when you take full responsibility for your life.

This doesn't mean blaming yourself for every obstacle or setback. It means recognizing that you have the power to change your circumstances by changing yourself. If you want better, you must become better. That starts with shifting your mindset, improving your habits, and making decisions that align with the future you want to create.

Taking responsibility for your growth means asking yourself tough questions: What am I doing that's holding me back? What habits need to change? Am I willing to do what's necessary to reach my goals?

This kind of introspection might be uncomfortable, but it's necessary. When you stop waiting for life to happen to you and start taking control of your actions, you'll notice that change begins to happen naturally.

Challenge Your Thought Patterns

The first step in reprogramming your subconscious is to challenge your current thought patterns. Start paying attention to the thoughts that run through your mind daily. Why do we talk like this? It's wild how we can dream big and want to achieve so much, but at the same time, we allow those conflicting thoughts to hold us back. At Pivot, I see this all the time. We have students walking through the door with untapped potential, but they've already placed limits on themselves based on what they've been told, or how they've been programmed to think. They're carrying around doubts that were never even theirs to begin with. And I get it I've been there, too.

The first step to breaking that cycle is to challenge those thoughts. Pay attention to the conversations happening in your own mind throughout the day. Are they lifting you up, or are they pulling you down? When you catch yourself thinking, "I can't do this," or "I'm not good enough," ask yourself: Who told me that? Is it actually true? This isn't just some cliché self-help advice it is real work. It's the difference between staying stuck or breaking free. Once you start questioning those limiting beliefs, you begin to realize that most of them are built on nothing but fear and assumptions. It's a simple practice, but it's powerful.

You must make it a habit to disrupt the negative dialogue going on in your head and take back control of your mindset.

Going through a divorce was one of the most gut-wrenching and painful moments of my life. More than anything, the feeling of having failed and knowing that I played a significant part in its end was overwhelming. But through time spent in introspection, in front of the mirror, and in moments of solitude, I've come to understand that the journey toward becoming the person I'm meant to be required facing those painful lessons head on.

Often, we resist growth and shy away from accountability, refusing to acknowledge the part we play in our own circumstances. Yet, the power to turn any situation around lies within us if we can push our thinking beyond our present state and embrace the changes we need to make.

I remember the moment when I first entered the tech world, sitting in rooms full of people who seemed to have it all figured out. I'd look around and feel like I was an imposter, like I didn't belong in those spaces. That same feeling came up when Josh and I began talking about building Pivot Tech. There were days I'd think, "Are we really the ones to pull this off? Can two guys from Nashville, without all the resources and connections, create a tech school that could truly make an impact?" I'd have these conversations in my head, questioning whether we could achieve something so big, all because I had allowed imposter syndrome to cloud my belief in what we could accomplish.

These doubts weren't confined to my professional life. As a husband and father, I had moments where I questioned whether I could truly be the man my family needed. I began focusing on what I was thinking, I understood the power of my thoughts to either build me up or break me down. Through this process, I've learned to intentionally choose empowering thoughts over those that are self-limiting.

So much of what holds us back is rooted in fear and insecurity. We fear failure, rejection, or embarrassment, so we play it safe. But playing it safe doesn't lead to growth but instead stagnation. And if you're not growing, you're not moving toward the life you want.

Once you identify those limiting thoughts, start replacing them with empowering ones. Reframe your thoughts, and over time, you'll reprogram your subconscious to support your success rather than sabotage it.

Focus on the Journey, Not the Destination

"But every 5 sit-ups, you tryna measure the progress."

It's human nature to want quick results. We want to see progress immediately, and when we don't, we start to doubt ourselves.

One of the biggest traps people fall into is expecting instant success without putting in the time and effort required to see real change, but success, growth, and mastery are all about the process, not the destination.

Think about it: When you're training for a marathon, you don't measure your success by how you feel after the first mile. You know it's about building endurance, pushing through the challenges, and putting in consistent effort over time. That same approach applies to your career, your personal growth, or your relationships. Long-term success is the result of small, intentional actions, repeated day after day, even when the finish line feels far off.

"I'm spending less energy on it if I ain't affecting it."

These lyrics speaks to the importance of directing your energy wisely. How often do we get caught up in things that don't move us closer to our goals? We spend time worrying about what other people think, scrolling through social media, or comparing ourselves to others, when that energy could be better spent focusing on what truly matters.

Momentum is built through action. But not just any action it takes focused, intentional action that aligns with your goals. Instead of worrying about how far you must go, focus on the steps you can take today. What can you do right now that will move you closer to where you want to be? It doesn't have to be a giant leap; just one small step is enough to build momentum.

The more you focus on the process, the less you'll worry about the end result. And paradoxically, that's when the results start to come. When you're fully immersed in the journey, when you're committed to the work, the success takes care of itself.

Big Stepper Energy: Thinking Beyond the Present

"My overnight success been literally 20 years straight."

One of the biggest misconceptions about success is that it happens overnight. But anyone who has achieved anything worthwhile will tell you that there's no such thing as an "overnight" success. Success is the result of years of hard work, persistence, and resilience. It's built on countless small steps, on the failures that taught you lessons, and on the moments when you wanted to quit but kept going anyway.

Embracing Pivotal Thoughts is about recognizing that the journey takes time. It's about thinking beyond your present circumstances and believing that something greater is possible, even when the odds seem stacked against you.

I remember being on a panel once where someone asked how we managed to make Pivot so successful in just three years. I paused for a moment, thinking about the question, and I laughed to myself. Three years? This has been a 20-year process. Everything I've learned over the years, whether it was building my own studio at 19 to record my music, or navigating supply and demand has compounded to get me to where I am today.

I started a cleaning business years ago, and I had no idea how to manage my employees, handle payroll, or secure more contracts. That experience, which some might call a failure, taught me more about operations than I could have ever imagined. Every "failure" along the way wasn't really a failure; it was preparation. Each step, even the missteps, equipped me with the knowledge and resilience to be ready for the next endeavor. That's the truth about success it's rarely about one big moment. It's about the accumulation of everything you've learned, every mistake and win, that prepares you for what's next.

Comfortable Being Uncomfortable

"And life has shown me with dead weight, it's too heavy to lift it."

Dead weight whether it's the negative beliefs we carry, the habits that don't serve us, or the relationships that drain us keeps us from moving forward. But sometimes, we hold onto that weight because it's familiar, because it's comfortable. Letting go means stepping into the unknown, and for many, that's a terrifying prospect. But here's the truth: growth doesn't happen in your comfort zone. Growth happens in the uncomfortable spaces, in the moments when you push past what feels safe and familiar to reach for something bigger.

One of the most powerful shifts you can make is learning to become comfortable with discomfort. Discomfort is a sign that you're stretching beyond your current limits, that you're expanding into new territory. And while it may feel unsettling at first, it's where the magic happens.

Think about it: every major achievement in your life probably came with some level of discomfort. Whether it was learning a new skill, navigating a difficult relationship, or taking a leap of faith in your career, the moments that challenged you the most were likely the ones that led to the most growth.

"*I suggest you evaluate who you are connected with it.*"

Who you surround yourself with matters. Your circle influences your thoughts, your actions, and ultimately, your success. If you're connected to people who don't support your growth, who don't believe in your vision, or who drain your energy, it's time to reevaluate those connections. Surround yourself with people who challenge you, who push you to be better, and who support your journey.

Your environment plays a huge role in shaping your mindset. If you're surrounded by negativity or people who don't believe in you, it's hard to maintain a positive, growth-oriented mindset. But when you surround yourself with people who uplift you, who encourage you to think bigger, who remind you of your potential, you create an environment that fosters success.

Take a moment to reflect on your relationships. Are the people in your life helping you grow, or are they holding you back? Are they encouraging your dreams, or are they feeding your doubts? Sometimes, the hardest but most necessary step is letting go of the people who no longer align with the future you're building.

You Are the CEO of Your Life

"I route it for the score, and they coming to interfere late."

This is about owning your story. It's about not letting other people interfere with your goals or dictate how you should live your life. You have the power to write your own narrative and decide who you want to be, what you want to achieve, and how you're going to get there.

Too often, we let other people's opinions influence our decisions. We worry about what they'll think if we fail, or we try to fit into the mold of what society expects from us. But the truth is, no one else is living your life. No one else has to deal with the consequences of your choices. So why should their opinions matter?

When you take ownership of your life you free yourself from the limitations that other people try to place on you. You stop seeking validation from others, and you start living according to your own values and beliefs.

Rewriting your narrative doesn't mean ignoring the past or pretending that your challenges don't exist. It means choosing how you respond to those challenges. It means deciding that, no matter what obstacles you face, you have the power to create a life that's meaningful and fulfilling.

Next, think about the habits or beliefs that have been holding you back. These could be old thought patterns, fears, or routines that no longer serve you. Choose one to focus on and make a conscious decision to replace it with a habit or mindset that aligns with your new, bigger vision. The goal is to start building momentum, to experience the power of your thoughts in action, and to see how, step by step, you can switch the algorithm of your life.

How You Can Change Your Algorithm

Changing your mental algorithm requires deliberate effort, but it's something you can start today by implementing a few key steps. The process of reprogramming your mind is about shifting your daily habits, your thought patterns, and the way you approach life. Here are three actionable steps to get you started:

1. Challenge Your Automatic Thoughts

   Begin by paying close attention to the automatic thoughts that run through your mind daily. Whenever you catch yourself thinking limiting thoughts ask yourself is this really true, or is it just a story I've been telling myself? Replace those thoughts with empowering ones.

2. Surround Yourself with Growth-Minded People

   Take a hard look at your current circle and ask whether they're pushing you to be better or keeping you stuck. Actively seek out individuals who challenge you, who have achieved what you aspire to, and who genuinely support your journey. Spend more time with people who inspire you to think bigger and do better. This energy will help elevate your mindset and push you toward success.

3. Create Daily Intentions and Stick to Them

   Set daily intentions that align with your goals. Whether it's taking small actions toward a larger career goal or improving your mindset through meditation or reading, make sure your actions reflect where you want to go. By setting intentions every day, you rewire your mind to focus on progress and growth, which will gradually shift your mental algorithm from limitation to possibility.

(1)

CHAPTER THREE

Too Many Followers

"In a culture of noise and influence, leadership comes from standing in your authenticity".

Link to Song: Too Many Followers

I remember one day, my son looked up at me and asked, "Daddy, how many followers do you have on Instagram?" It caught me off guard, not because of the question, but because of what it represented. In that moment, my mind drifted to how we live in a world obsessed with followers, with influence, with the numbers that seem to define our worth. But the real question is how much of our lives actually match what we portray on social media? How many of us are living lives that are more filtered than the pictures we post?

Today it seems we've become so focused on what's trending that we've lost sight of what truly matters like our values, our integrity, and our ability to develop leaders. We have created a world where everyone is chasing facades and it's easier than ever to get caught up in the noise.

The Seduction of Superficial Success

Here's the thing; Today it seems there are more influencers than there are people to influence. The algorithm has been designed to reward an ability to distract and predict behavior. One of the best strategies is the constant allure of instant gratification. Social media has been programmed to discourage authenticity or content that may foster low engagement. Therefore, our timelines are redundant messaging meant to turn us into addicted consumers.

"Was so enthused to prove myself—leave my mark on the game; multifaceted brain, their mental ain't ever the same."

I've always been driven by a passion to motivate, build a brand, and leave a legacy. I used to measure my success by the thigs I was able to accomplish. I've realized that chasing external validation was pulling me away from my true purpose. The more I tried to fit into what others expected, the more I felt like I was losing myself. My mind, my creativity those are my real gifts, and they can't thrive in a space where I'm constantly trying to fit into someone else's mold.

There was a time when I was determined to be the greatest rapper to ever come out of Nashville. I pushed myself hard, always chasing perfection, convinced that every verse, every beat had to show everyone I was the best. That drive followed me when I stepped into tech. I was so focused on moving up, proving myself in an entirely new field, that I didn't take a moment to appreciate the journey or acknowledge what I was building. I was locked into this mindset of constant pressure, more focused on the climb than on the growth unfolding right in front of me.

What I've come to understand is that real success isn't about constantly proving yourself to others; it's about staying true to who you are and using your unique abilities to make an impact. That need to prove something often leads you to paths that aren't meant for you. It becomes a distraction, pulling you away from your authentic journey. The key is recognizing this early and being willing to pivot, to shift your energy toward what truly matters and where you can make the most meaningful progress.

The Cost of Conformity

"I see too many followers, aye, tell me where the leaders at"

We've become a society that values conformity over originality, and the cost of this is immeasurable. When everyone is following the same trends, the same ideas, the same leaders, we lose the diversity of thought and creativity that drives progress. We end up in an echo chamber where the loudest voices drown out the most important ones.

One of the key principles I teach my kids is that a true leader is always two steps ahead of the followers. There's a reason some people seem to have motion, no matter where they are. This principle isn't just about social media, even though that's where it's most visible; it's about life itself.

We've grown so comfortable following trends and crowds that we've forgotten how to think independently, how to move in a way that reflects our unique path. It's easier to go with the flow, but what we gain in acceptance, we lose in authenticity.

I've seen it in business and across industries, people who could create powerful alliances choosing competition over collaboration, missing the real potential that comes from working together. In their rush to one-up each other, they overlook the depth and patience it takes to build something that lasts. It's as if everyone is focused on winning their own race, without realizing that true impact often requires us to set ego aside and invest in the bigger picture.

The truth is, we limit ourselves when we think too small, driven by short-term wins or the need to prove something. But the real breakthroughs happen when we embrace the power of collaboration, of bringing our unique strengths together to build something far more significant than any individual success. Growth isn't found in mimicking others or just fitting in it comes from owning who we are, taking risks, and knowing that sometimes, the best moves come when we rise above competition to create something meaningful. Standing out isn't always easy, but that's where the real value lies.

When you dare to lead instead of follow, you unlock your creativity, tap into your true potential, and pave the way for something extraordinary.

The temporary discomfort of stepping outside the box is nothing compared to the empowerment that comes from living authentically and owning your individuality.

Building on a Foundation of Values

One of the most important lessons I've learned is that leadership must be built on a solid foundation of values. Without this, leadership is just a façade that will crumble at the first sign of trouble.

"I try to see the best; my environment inspires me to stretch; 300 push-ups no less, discipline in the flesh."

We live in a time where society has gradually eroded its value system, and the effects of this shift are undeniable. What once grounded us, honesty, integrity, accountability, and respect have become blurred in a world where almost anything goes. As a result, many people don't know who they are, what they stand for, or who they should aspire to be. The lines between right and wrong, success and failure, real and fake, are now so thin that people are left questioning the very foundations upon which we once built our lives.

The Information Age has essentially become the algorithm we need to switch. It's an age where information, rather than empowering us, often leaves us feeling more uncertain, as if we're living in some kind of matrix. The sheer volume of conflicting information being fed to us at every moment has created a society where truth is subjective, and values are malleable. What was once understood to be real or valuable is constantly being challenged, leaving people in a state of confusion. We are bombarded with different versions of "success" and "happiness" from social media, marketing, and influencers who often present lifestyles that are at odds with the deeper values that lead to fulfillment. With everything appearing acceptable, the clarity of purpose that values once provided has been diluted.

This lack of a solid value system has led to a loss of identity for many. People are constantly changing who they are to fit into the latest trends, seeking validation from external sources rather than being grounded in who they truly are. The result is a society full of followers, and people who move with the crowd rather than creating their own path based on principles that endure.

True discipline separates talent from greatness. It's not about showing up once or even for one season; it's about committing every single day, regardless of the applause or the setbacks. Leaders who consistently rise to the top have an unshakable dedication to their vision. They show us that success isn't built on shortcuts or following trends but staying true to the process and being relentless in the pursuit of something real.

Discipline isn't just hard work; it's staying anchored to your values even when the world is shifting around you. Leaders like LeBron James, who has demonstrated focus and resilience season after season, or entrepreneurs like Steve Jobs, who stayed committed to his vision even when it wasn't popular, remind us what true leadership looks like. They set the bar for standing firm in a world that constantly pushes us to drift. These leaders didn't become who they are by chasing what was easy or trendy; they stayed committed to a purpose that transcended any momentary success. Real leadership isn't about fitting in or riding the wave it's about creating one.

In a world where values are treated as temporary, real leadership is about standing firm with purpose. It's about creating impact that goes beyond the moment, building a legacy that lasts in a society hungry for something real.

Superficial Leadership

Superficial leadership thrives because so many are searching without a true foundation. When people lack a clear sense of purpose, they're easily swayed by what looks good on the surface. Real leadership, though, requires depth and integrity. It challenges people to think critically and build their own values rather than just following trends. Authentic leaders don't just attract attention; they create lasting impact by staying rooted in substance. It's this kind of leadership that doesn't fade but endures, grounded in something real.

"I'm socially so opposed to posing when he get dressed; I'd be impressed if your jewelry's less than what you invest."

My favorite rapper J. Cole's verse on "Port Antonio" cuts deep into the reality of our obsession with social media validation and the emptiness behind it. When he says, "I wouldn't have lost a battle, dawg, I would have lost a bro," he's confronting the cost of giving in to petty competition and ego-driven fights. It's easy to get caught up in proving something, in thinking that another "win" will somehow make us feel whole. But, as he points out, it would have just gained him an enemy and lost him a friend, all for some "props from strangers that do not have a clue what I been aiming' for."

It's a question of integrity over popularity and being who we really are versus who we perform as online. The "algorithm-bots" Cole references are symbolic of people who live purely for online approval, swaying their actions and beliefs to fit whatever's trending or profitable.

It's a trap that makes it easy to confuse validation with value. Cole's choice to walk away from all that shows the real strength it takes to stay grounded in a world that's constantly pulling us into superficial battles.

This is just another reminder that clout can never equal purpose. The approval we chase online is like the stock market. One day we are up, the very next day there is a sudden drop, and we can never fill the deeper need we all have to do something meaningful. Real success isn't about flexing for followers or tearing someone down to prove your worth. It's about building a life that's authentic and connected to something larger than yourself.

Superficial leadership might get you attention in the short term, but it won't sustain you in the long term. Eventually, the façade will crack, and the truth will come out.

That's why it's so important to focus on the things that really matter. The real value happens when you invest in yourself, in your growth, in your values, rather than in the things that make you look good on the surface. True leadership is about depth, not superficiality. It's about substance, not style.

The Power of Authenticity

One of the most powerful lessons I've learned is the importance of authenticity.

"My sentiments, them filters still reveal that you ain't changed."

This line speaks to the heart of what it means to be authentic in a world that's obsessed with appearances. Filters might hide your flaws, but they can't change who you are. Authenticity is about being true to yourself, about showing the world who you really are, without pretense or deception.

Authenticity is rare in a world where everyone is trying to be something they're not. But it's also incredibly powerful. When you're authentic, you inspire others to be authentic as well. You create a space where people can be themselves, where they don't have to pretend, where they can find their own path rather than following someone else's. This is the kind of leadership that changes lives, that builds communities, that creates lasting impact.

Being authentic isn't always easy. It requires vulnerability, the willingness to show your flaws, to admit your mistakes, to be real in a world that often rewards the opposite. But I've found that the more authentic I am, the more connected I feel to myself and to others. Authenticity builds trust, and trust is the foundation of any successful relationship, whether it's in business, in family, or in friendship.

Leading by Example

Leadership isn't just about words; it's about actions. It's about embodying the values you believe in and leading by example for others to follow.

"I been on interventions, like building my family business; employing my children; yeah, I been implementing what I mention."

This line highlights the significance of embodying your principles, making sure your actions consistently align with what you believe in across all areas of your life.

For me, this has meant not just talking about leadership, but living it. It's meant making tough decisions, taking risks, and staying true to my principles, even when it would have been easier to follow the crowd. It's meant building a business that reflects my values, one that has empowered me to hire my son, provides opportunities for others, and makes a positive impact on the world. And it's meant showing my children what it means to be a leader, not just telling them.

Leading by example is one of the most powerful ways to inspire others. When people see you living your values, they're more likely to follow your lead. When people see you living your truth, they're more inclined to trust you, to believe in what you stand for, and to feel genuinely inspired by your journey. In a world where so many are searching for real direction, this type of authentic leadership matters now more than ever.

The Challenge leading today

Leading in today's world is complex, not just because of the pace of life but because of the constant barrage of narratives designed to distract us from our core. Social media glorifies instant success, material wealth, and superficial markers of achievement. It paints a picture that says, "You should have more," "You should be more," and "You're falling behind if you're not keeping up." These narratives are subtle but powerful, pulling you in with promises of validation and applause. It's easy to be seduced by the idea that your worth is tied to how many followers you have, how perfectly curated your life looks, or how closely you align with the latest trend. But this is a false blueprint, one that leads to a hollow version of success.

Maintaining discipline in this environment requires you to be intentional about how you engage with the world. It starts with clarity—

knowing who you are and what you stand for. This isn't just about a surface-level understanding of your values; it's about a deep connection to your purpose, one that's not swayed by external noise. Discipline looks like setting boundaries for yourself, both mentally and physically. It's about consciously choosing what you consume, whether it's the media you watch, the people you interact with, or the content you allow to shape your thoughts.

Real discipline means creating space for reflection, where you regularly check in with yourself: Are your actions aligned with your long-term goals, or are you getting pulled off track by temporary distractions? It's about not just saying "no" to what doesn't serve you, but also consistently saying "yes" to the habits, routines, and environments that support your growth. That might mean waking up earlier to work on personal goals, limiting screen time, or surrounding yourself with people who push you to think bigger and stay grounded.

In the end, discipline is about having the courage to move against the current. It's about choosing the path of consistent effort and deliberate action over the path of least resistance. It's realizing that true leadership isn't about being everything to everyone—it's about being unwaveringly yourself in a world that's constantly trying to make you someone else.

"I peeped how the game played, you quit cause' you can't dream then see it all in the same day."

We've become a society addicted to quick fixes, chasing shortcuts over long-term solutions. We lean towards Ozempic instead of committing to exercise and healthy habits, hoping for instant results. We'd rather gamble than invest, looking for a windfall instead of building wealth slowly over time. We buy into credit hacks, desperate to improve our situation overnight, and cling to a lottery mentality, convinced that our big break is just one lucky moment away. But these shortcuts come at a cost.

The truth is, we've been sold a dream by those who exploit our impatience and desire for immediate success. They profit from our unwillingness to invest in the process, to do the hard work that leads to lasting change. It's time we reclaim our power, reject the quick fixes, and understand that true success requires discipline, patience, and a commitment to the journey.

Leadership today requires the ability to think long-term, to see beyond the immediate rewards, to stay focused on your vision even when the world around you is changing rapidly. It requires the ability to adapt, to pivot, to find new ways to achieve your goals without compromising your values. And it requires the courage to stand alone, to lead when no one else is following, to stay true to your principles even when it's difficult.

Reclaiming Leadership in a World of Followers

We live in a world where followers outnumber leaders. It's easier to follow than to lead, to go along with the crowd rather than to stand out. But I believe that we all have the capacity to be leaders, to make a difference, to live a life that's true to our values. It's not about being the loudest voice in the room; it's about being the most authentic, the most disciplined, the most consistent.

Real leadership is more than just a title, an image, or the number of followers someone has. Facade leaders are everywhere—people who look the part but lack the depth, those who promise quick solutions but don't have the substance to back it up.

But then there are real leaders, the ones who don't need to shout because their actions speak for them. Nipsey Hussle introduced the world to "The Marathon," a mindset focused on enduring the process, staying committed even when success seems far off. Nipsey's life and music taught us that progress isn't overnight, that true change is a product of consistency and discipline, not shortcuts.

Growing up, my grandfather was the first real example of a black entrepreneur I could look up to. He owned a grocery store and a department store, something you didn't see a lot of in our community. I didn't fully grasp it at the time but watching him work showed me what true leadership looked like. He was respected because he was consistent, dependable, and committed to building something that benefited not only his family but also the entire neighborhood. Leadership was about showing up every day, doing the work, and serving others.

The truth is young people today are incredibly impressionable. They are watching us, whether we realize it or not, and they will follow whoever they see themselves in. If they don't have to model resilience, integrity, and work ethic, they're going to be influenced by whoever gives them attention, even if that person is leading them down the wrong path.

That's why genuine leadership is so important right now. Young people need to see that success isn't about quick wins or instant recognition. It's about building something real and lasting, something with depth and purpose. My grandfather showed me what was possible, and we owe it to the next generation to do the same: lead with purpose, build with integrity, and show them a blueprint for real success.

'Too many followers' is a call to action, a challenge to switch the algorithm that governs our lives, to step away from the crowd and take a stand for something real. The world needs genuine leaders now more than ever. The question is are you ready to rise to the challenge?

How You Can Change Your Algorithm

In a world where values are constantly shifting and conflicting information is everywhere, it's more important than ever to take control of your personal "algorithm." This is about the habits, thoughts, and influences that shape your life. Here are three actionable steps to help you realign with your core values and step into leadership:

1. Clarify Your Values

    Take time to reflect on what truly matters to you. Ask yourself: *What are the non-negotiable principles I want to live by?* When faced with choices, refer back to these values to guide you. This will help you stay consistent and avoid being swayed by trends or external pressure

2. Audit Your Influences

    Evaluate who and what you're allowing into your space. It's time to unfollow those who encourage a lifestyle that conflicts with your principles and surround yourself with content and people that uplift and challenge you to be better. This creates a positive algorithm that reinforces the person you want to become.

3. Practice Consistency in Small Actions

    True leadership is built on consistency. Start with small, daily actions that align with your values. Being consistent builds trust within yourself and with others. Remember, leadership is about consistently doing the right thing, even when no one is watching.

CHAPTER FOUR

50/50

"Partnerships are built on synergy, not competition. Don't be fooled by those who've never done it".

Link to Song: 50-50

Disclaimer: Coach Q is not a relationship advisor, counselor, or therapist. I am not qualified to give relationship advice, and you should NOT make any decisions based on my views, thoughts, or beliefs. Now, back to our regularly scheduled programming.

I honestly don't know how the 50/50 conversation became *the* topic that makes people lose their minds on the internet. Part of me thinks it's just boredom and our tendency to feed on anything toxic or divisive for entertainment. But another part of me believes this narrative was fed into our community on purpose. People know how easily distracted we are when we're constantly in-fighting, bickering over roles and expectations, instead of focusing on real partnership, building legacy, and community growth.

I watched my grandfather provide for my grandmother while running a couple of stores, managing their partnership, and staying married for over 50 years. I also saw my mom and stepdad, Kenny, both work and support each other, building a marriage that has lasted over 27 years. I've witnessed the full spectrum, from people who have everything provided for them but feel like they've lost their sense of identity and purpose to others who are completely fulfilled through mutual support. On the flip side, I've seen countless single individuals on the internet offering relationship advice that doesn't reflect real-life dynamics. What I've realized is that the only relationship model that truly works is the one that works for *you* and the person you're with. The truth is there's no universal blueprint for success.

The internet is flooded with "gurus" and podcasters dissecting every aspect of relationships, especially in our culture. What's troubling is that many of these conversations push an algorithm of opposition rather than one of collaboration. They create this toxic dynamic, constantly pitting men and women against each other. It's like we've embraced a narrative of competition and distrust instead of focusing on collaboration and growth.

This mindset has infiltrated our communities, shaping expectations and reinforcing stereotypes that only serve to divide us.

The conversation has shifted from building healthy partnerships to a battle of egos. But we need to understand who we are and what our culture has always been built on. Our strength has always come from unity, from building each other up and creating strong family foundations. Yet somehow, we're now in the middle of a civil war happening inside our own homes. It's like we know what's at the root of this dynamic, but we can't seem to shake the appeal of the algorithm that pits us against each other.

We recognize how these conversations are dividing us, yet we keep getting drawn in, allowing this false narrative to dismantle what's meant to hold us together: our partnerships, our families, our community.

Instead of focusing on how we can grow and complement each other, we've turned the dialogue into a contest of blame and division. What could be an opportunity to learn how to create stronger, more fulfilling partnerships has become a platform for tearing each other apart.

These discussions shouldn't just be about who pays the bills or meets certain expectations—it's about where we invest our attention, energy, and values. Social media has shifted the narrative, making relationships seem like a battleground instead of a space for mutual support and growth. The real question is: who benefits from these constant debates? Certainly not us. Our community is being led away from unity and progress when we allow these conversations to be divisive.

"Let's shoot out the city baby... yea we way too busy."

Toxic Quick Fixes

One of the things I've come to understand is that a lot of men, especially young boys, are set up for failure from the start. Due to a lack of proper parenting, too many young men aren't given the foundation and principles needed to develop discipline, resilience, and resourcefulness. They're sent into adulthood without the tools they need to succeed. For many men, real adulthood doesn't begin to click until they hit 30 or even later.

By then, society expects them to already be equipped to provide for a family, to lead, and to shoulder responsibilities. The reality is that they're still learning on the job, often struggling because they've never been properly taught.

One of the hardest lessons I had to learn was that I simply wasn't ready to be a husband and lead a family when I thought I was. The weight of that realization was tough, but it opened my eyes. Those life lessons now fuel the way I guide my sons, making sure they understand that becoming a capable and resourceful man doesn't happen by chance; it requires hard work, self-reflection, and a commitment to growth. I teach them that if they want to lead a family, they must first lead themselves with integrity and discipline.

At the same time, I show my daughter that her value as a woman doesn't lie in her beauty or in some automatic entitlement. She's learning that, like anyone else, she has to put in the work to acquire the things she wants in life.

I believe that the root of this issue—this gap between expectation and readiness—comes from unmet love, false expectations, unresolved trauma, deep emotional voids, and a lot of misinformation. We've inherited a cycle that can only be broken by stepping up, doing the hard work, and creating a new narrative for ourselves and the generations that follow.

We're constantly bombarded with messages about what relationships *should* look like, what success *should* feel like, and what happiness *should* mean. It's all designed to make us feel like we're falling short and need to spend more, do more, and be more in order to measure up. But the real cost is our happiness and the health of our relationships. We're so caught up in what we think we're supposed to be that we forget to simply *be*.

Comparison - Death of all things great

We constantly feel like we're missing out. The internet is designed to make us believe that whatever we have or are doing right now isn't enough. It's wild how we can be on vacation, in the middle of what should be a relaxing or joyful moment, and as soon as we see someone else's post, we start questioning why we aren't where they are. Suddenly, the joy of our experience fades, and we're wondering why we don't have the new truck or why we're working while others seem to be living the life we think we deserve. But the truth is, we're being bombarded with carefully curated moments snapshots of someone's life that either aren't real or show only a sliver of the whole picture. And yet, we compare, we question, and we feel less than, all based on an illusion.

What we see is the highlight reel, and when we compare it to our own lives, it leaves us feeling like we're not doing enough. This obsession with comparison can rob us of joy in the present moment and cloud our judgment about what's truly important. It tricks us into thinking that we're behind when in reality everyone is on their own unique journey.

The 80-20 rule always seems to show us that 20 percent we think we're missing at just the right time, tapping into our insecurities and fueling the idea that something better is out there. The danger lies in the fact that our minds aren't designed to handle temptations and distractions 24 hours a day. Social media and constant exposure to everyone else's highlight reels make it impossible to avoid falling into the comparison trap.

We've all been there. The problem arises when we start letting those comparisons overshadow what we have. Instead of appreciating our own relationships, we begin to view them through a lens of inadequacy. It's easy to convince ourselves that someone else could offer something better or that we deserve more without considering the real effort and commitment it takes to build something lasting. We start thinking that if we just found someone different, everything would magically fall into place. But the reality is that no one is perfect, and no relationship is effortlessly magical. Everything takes work, patience, and a willingness to see beyond the illusion of perfection that the world constantly tries to sell us.

Everybody has the answers

We must manage our intrusive thoughts, the ones that pull us into doubt and lead us to believe that we're in competition with each other rather than in collaboration. We buy into the idea being sold to us that a relationship is a transaction, a checklist, a set of obligations instead of a partnership, and we end up feeling empty.

We need to refocus our energy and recognize that the most powerful presence is a black man and women unified. There is immense power in working together, in aligning our values and understanding that the best relationships are built on balance. This doesn't mean that balance looks the same for everyone because every couple will have a different equation. But what's important is that both sides bring their best selves to the table. This means not expecting your partner to fix what you haven't worked on within yourself or looking for someone to make you whole. It's about coming together as two solid, complete individuals, ready to build something bigger and better together than either of you could on your own.

The Real Cost of 50/50 Thinking

"They can't compare 'cause Instagram don't ever see what we been on / It's all division, most these podcasters' house ain't even home."

Conversations about masculine and feminine energy, and the growing trend of the "soft life," have sparked debates, but often without a full understanding of what it truly means. While I was in the studio working on "50/50," we started having a deep conversation about the concepts behind the song. What hit us was the realization that a lot of the expectations we have around relationships and finances come from a conceptual place, not a practical one. Take Nashville, for example where the cost of living is out of control. There are very few people who can provide for an entire family on a single income while still having enough left over to save, invest, and enjoy life. But despite these realities, many of us still hold onto these ideals about how things *should* be, regardless of the facts.

The truth is, in many situations, if we came together as partners and laid everything on the table, we could map out the life we both desire. It doesn't always have to be a one-size-fits-all approach. Together, we can design the life we want to live, but it requires open communication, collaboration, and the willingness to set aside the societal pressures telling us what's right or wrong. Instead of living by unrealistic standards, we can build a reality that works for both partners. The truth is most of the loudest voices on this subject aren't coming from places of genuine understanding. Many of them speak from a platform that isn't built on real-life experiences but rather on curated, commercialized narratives designed to gain attention. We scroll through our timelines, seeing couples posing in perfect harmony, and we compare that to our own struggles.

But what we see on social media is often just a snapshot. Social media creates an illusion of perfection that doesn't show the work behind it, the sacrifices made, or the disagreements resolved

It doesn't show the nights spent in deep conversation, trying to figure out the path forward together.

This push for "50/50" has become a tool of division, and we have to ask ourselves who benefits when we're divided? Who profits from a community of people who are constantly at odds, trying to prove their independence, instead of working together toward something greater?

The Mindset of Division vs. Building Together

"But see the energy they feeding got us playing enemies / I'm tryna intervene so we can focus on some chemistry."

The mindset of division is destructive. It keeps us looking at each other as competitors rather than partners.

It makes us keep a tally of every contribution and every sacrifice, rather than recognizing that love and partnership are not about keeping score.

They're about giving freely and trusting that the other person is doing the same. When we buy into the mindset of division, we begin to see our partner as someone we have to outdo or prove ourselves against, rather than someone we are working alongside.

Creating a Legacy Together

"Let's leave the city, lease another yacht, and dock at Venice Beach / And talk about the life we need, What's a team without the Queen."

Have you ever wondered why we hold onto certain beliefs about relationships without really questioning where they came from? A lot of us grow up seeing relationships that don't work the way we think they should, and we tell ourselves, "I'm not going to end up like that." We reject the patterns we saw in our parents or those around us, convinced that we'll do it better or differently. But we rarely stop to consider *why* they made the choices they made, or what pressures and sacrifices shaped their decisions.

I used to think the same way. Growing up, I saw relationships that seemed more about survival than love and witnessed people just trying to make it through. I told myself I wouldn't follow that path, that I'd find a way to create something different, something better. But as I started building my own partnerships, I began to realize that judging what you don't fully understand is easy. I didn't have the full picture of what it took to stay in a relationship for 30, 40 years. I didn't understand the sacrifices, the compromises, and the deep commitment required to make something last that long.

We often avoid advice from those who have been in long-lasting marriages, thinking their ways are outdated or irrelevant today.

It is very possible that they understood something we don't. Relationships aren't built on instant gratification or 50/50 splits, but on resilience and long-term vision. It's not about settling, but about understanding that real love is a marathon, not a sprint. So, why do we shy away from the wisdom of those who've walked the road before us?

Are we so focused on doing things our way that we're missing out on the lessons that could help us build something lasting and real? It's time to ask ourselves: are we rejecting their experience, or are we afraid of the kind of commitment it takes to build the legacy we say we want? It's time to move beyond the toxicity and start having conversations that heal, that uplift, and that allow us to build the kind of relationships we all deserve. Conversations that are about partnership, about growth, about seeing each other's value and understanding that we are stronger together than we are apart. This is the real 50/50. It's a partnership that's built on mutual respect, equal investment, and a shared vision for the future.

How You Can Change Your Algorithm: 50/50

1. Have Real Conversations

   Get past surface-level talks. Sit down with your partner and discuss your real goals, values, and challenges. Make sure you're on the same page about what works for your relationship, not what others expect.

2. Define Your Own Blueprint

   Stop measuring your relationship by social media standards or other people's opinions. Focus on what success looks like for both of you and create a plan that fits your unique situation.

3. Work on Yourself

   Your relationship can't grow if you're not growing. Address any personal challenges, traumas, or unmet needs, so you can show up as your best self and contribute fully to the partnership.

CHAPTER FIVE

Girl Dad/MANnerisms

"Nothing in life creates the avenues to grow like fatherhood".

"Who am I to be so lucky to have you / A rare jewel that is too precious to value."

July 5, May 7, August 13, and May 31st are four dates that hold more weight than anything else in my world. Sometimes, I think God knew I needed my kids as much as they needed me. They gave me a reason, a "why," to push past where I was and transform into who I was meant to be. Fatherhood is deeply transformative, especially when you're raising daughters. "Girl Dad" is something I am beyond proud to call myself. Being a father to a daughter carries a responsibility that reshaped how I view love, family, and my own purpose in life.

From the moment I held my daughter, I knew she was going to completely change me as person. She's been far more than just my daughter; she's been my mirror, my lesson, and my drive to evolve. Raising a daughter been a journey that's reshaped me as a man, pushing me to redefine what strength, patience, and love truly means. She's taught me that being a father isn't just about providing or protecting. Fatherhood is also about constantly becoming better, for her and for myself. In her eyes, I see the future I'm responsible for shaping, and that reality keeps me striving to grow every single day.

As fathers, we often don't get the recognition for the emotional work we do, but that doesn't lessen the importance of our role. In fact, we are the first men in our daughters' lives, shaping their understanding of love, respect, and connection with men as they grow.

Our presence, or lack thereof, plays a significant role in shaping how they navigate the world. That's why we must be intentional about the love we give and the lessons we teach. Our daughters benefit tremendously from having a loving father who provides emotional safety, financial stability, and a strong foundation for how to move through life.

"You taught me how to love more delicate / Yeah baby, you're my subject and the predicate."

Becoming a father to a daughter forced me into a level of emotional maturity I wasn't prepared for but definitely needed. With two sons at the time, I focused on discipline, structure, and being the example of a man, they could one day become. But having a daughter opened a new chapter in my journey. This chapter demanded I go beyond just being strong and protective. I had to develop emotional intelligence in ways I hadn't anticipated.

Raising a daughter required me to slow down, listen, and really engage with her emotions. She needed more than a provider; she needed someone who could help her navigate the complex emotions of being a black girl in this world. That meant I had to be emotionally available, not just physically present. I had to learn how to have conversations that weren't based on solving problems but simply being there for her, hearing her, and helping her feel understood.

Having my daughter didn't just make me a father it's what truly brought "Coach Q" to life. She became my mirror, reflecting back the areas where I was falling short, not only in leadership but also in my closest relationships. I realized that I'd been so focused on the grind, on achieving and pushing forward, that I hadn't fully shown up for the people I care about, especially in my intimate relationships. She showed me where I needed to slow down, listen, and actually feel what the people around me were going through.

Her influence helped me realize that the role of a leader isn't just to drive results; it's to connect, to be someone people feel they can trust and open up to. Coach Q was born from that shift, understanding that true strength is in creating balance, knowing when to push and when to simply be present. She taught me to bring that same focus on growth and honesty to my personal life, to be the kind of person who doesn't just show up in the big moments but in the everyday ways that actually matter.

My daughter has taught me that not every moment needs to be about guidance or life lessons. Sometimes, we just need to laugh, relax, and embrace the moment for what it is. Our connection is a reminder that being a father isn't always about teaching or leading but being truly being present. I never know when I am going to get one our facetimes, but it always seem to come at a time that grounds me. She's not just my daughter; she's her own incredible person, someone whose spirit has a way of bringing me back to what's real.

I didn't always understand the depth of my role as a father to my daughter; it's something I've learned through life, love, and plenty of forgiveness of myself and others. Over time, I realized that as fathers, we don't just influence how our daughters feel about others, but how they feel about themselves. Every FaceTime call I answer, every hug I give after a rough day, every moment I sit and really listen to her stories is a reminder that she's seen, she's heard, and valued. These small interactions create a foundation that helps her navigate life with strength and confidence. It's in these moments, I've come to see, that we show them they're worthy of love and respect, laying the groundwork for a resilience that runs deep.

Emotional Intelligence and Safety

In a world where social media constantly shapes self-image, our role as fathers has taken on a deeper level of importance. With so many outside influences that can distort our daughters' sense of self-worth, I've learned it is a father's job to reinforce their value from within. Being a father today means going beyond simply providing or protecting. It means teaching them how to navigate their emotions, communicate with confidence, and understand their true worth. We must show them that they're more than just what the world sees on a screen, grounding them in self-respect and resilience. This foundation is what helps them find strength in themselves, making sure they're equipped to face life with clarity and purpose, no matter the pressures around them.

"Keep your eyes on your feet, always know where you stand"

It's not always easy to show up with emotional maturity, especially when life pulls us in every direction. But I've come to believe that challenging ourselves in this area is essential. Our daughters don't just need us to be physically present they need us to be tuned in emotionally, to show them it's okay to feel deeply and handle those feelings with resilience. It's a continual process, one that demands intention and patience, but the impact it leaves on our daughters is worth every bit of effort. By providing that steady, safe space, we're equipping them with a foundation that will ground them, even when the rest of the world tries to shake their confidence.

The Role of Fathers

As a 20-year-old father, I felt the weight of responsibility to guide this young kid that looked at me for all the answers. I knew I needed to be there for him, to set an example, but I quickly realized I didn't have the tools to show him the way. I was barely learning what it meant to be a man myself, and here I was with a life depending on me to figure it out. My presence, my actions, and even my mistakes would become the blueprint he'd look to as he grew.

This is the gap I see in so many young men today. What is missing is the blueprint that should come from a principled father figure. Without that model, it's easy for boys to drift, to find themselves emulating influences that might look good on the surface but don't provide real guidance. That's why it's on us as fathers to step up, to be the stabilizing force in this world.

Now, I push myself to be that example every day. I don't just want to tell my sons what it means to be a man; I want to show them. I want them to see that manhood is built on purpose, consistency, and integrity. I want to give them a foundation they can rely on. I've worked to create a roadmap rooted in principles that will guide them long after I'm gone. For me, that's one of the most meaningful parts of fatherhood.

"What's up young Tez, you the prince in my mind / See you following my steps, left prints you can find."

Every time I sit across from my oldest son in a Pivot conference room, it feels like my own version of LeBron and Bronny hooping together in the NBA. Being able to bring my son into the business and watch him step into spaces I've helped build is one of my greatest highlights as a father. There's no pressure, no expectations—just genuine advice whenever he asks for it. What makes it even better is looking over and knowing we're reshaping our family's path, one meeting at a time. Seeing him there fuels me to keep building because it's not just about today; it's about setting up something real for the future, with him right by my side.

Raising sons is about so much more than just talking about success or strength; it's about showing them, day in and day out, what real manhood looks like. When I look at my sons, I see pieces of myself in how they carry themselves, the habits they're picking up, even the struggles they face. They're not just watching, they're absorbing, learning from every move I make. That reality pushes me to be intentional in everything I do. I'm setting the standard for them, whether it's in how I handle challenges or how I treat others. Knowing that keeps me focused on being the best version of myself; not just for me, but to give them a blueprint they can carry forward.

When my sons look at me, they see their future selves. They're picking up on how I treat people, how I handle adversity, how I love, and how I lead. If I want them to grow into men of honor, compassion, and strength, then I have to model those traits every single day. The values I instill in them will become the foundation they rely on as they make their way through life.

"Even your birthday is five days before mine"

Cydney and I have always been close, almost like a reflection of each other in so many ways. From the way he moves to how he thinks, it's clear that he's picked up so much of me. But one of the hardest parts of being his father is realizing that, despite our closeness, I have to give him room to grow into who *he* truly wants to be. As much as I want to protect him and guide him through every decision, I've had to learn that part of fatherhood is stepping back and trusting the foundation I've laid. It's recognizing that while he carries so much of me, his path is his own.

Even our birthdays are only five days apart, a constant reminder of how closely our lives are intertwined. But while those shared traits and moments bond us, it's through my boys that I realize the depth of the legacy I'm leaving behind. They're not just watching me but they are absorbing everything. The good habits, the strengths, and even the flaws I wish I could hide. That's the weight of fatherhood. You're not just raising kids; you're molding future men. Every action I take leaves a blueprint for them, and it constantly reminds me of the impact I have, even when I'm not speaking.

"*Young Lennox, you're my heart, you extended my life / You're the reason I fight, make sure dreams gon' ignite.*"

Watching Lennox grow has been a full-circle moment for me as a father. It's incredible to see how my three boys, despite sharing so many traits, each have their own unique paths. Lennox, being the youngest, has this energy and curiosity that brings me back to my own childhood. He's a constant reminder of how life evolves and how each of my sons, are carving out their own identities.

There's something about the youngest that brings you back to the "why" of it all. Lennox brought a wave of life and renewal into my world that I didn't expect but deeply needed. He gave me a fresh sense of freedom and focus that's helped me grow even more as a man. It's wild how your youngest child can open your eyes to things you didn't see before—he's shown me that fatherhood isn't just a role, it's an evolution. And with him, I'm constantly learning, constantly growing.

Lennox brings a whole different light into my life. I have realized this is not just because he's the youngest, but because he's deepened my perspective on what family and connection really mean. He's pushed me to see myself not only as a father but as a man, making me more intentional, more present, and more patient with all my kids. He's my reminder that every day holds a fresh chance to grow, not just in fatherhood, but in who I am.

When I look at Cydney, Cyntez, and Lennox together, it's like seeing pieces of myself in different stages of life. Each of them reflects a unique part of who I am, yet they're all so distinct. Lennox's energy, his curiosity, his pure joy all reminds me to stay open, to keep learning. Fatherhood isn't just about guiding them; it's about letting them guide me too. I'm realizing that they're teaching me as much as I'm teaching them, shaping who I am right alongside me.

Respect and Legacy

"Always love on your moms, she is always your Queen."

One of the most important lessons I want to impart to my sons is the value of loving and showing respect to their mother. It's about them understanding that love isn't just something you say, it's something you show through your actions, every single day. I want them to see how I treat their mom with kindness and care because that's how I want them to treat the women in their lives.

The legacy we leave behind isn't just in our accomplishments; it's in the values we instill in our children. It's in the love we show, the respect we demand, and the strength we demonstrate. Our children are watching, absorbing everything we do, and they will carry those lessons with them long after we're gone.

Foundations That Carry On

The roles fathers play in their children's lives are often minimized, but they are vital. Our actions, our presence, and our ability to be there in both the big and small moments lay the foundation for our children's sense of self. Whether it's the love we show our daughters, ensuring they know their worth, or the example we set for our sons, teaching them how to navigate the world with both strength and compassion, our influence is immeasurable.

We are creating a legacy that will carry on for generations. We are setting the standard for how our daughters will allow themselves to be treated, and we're showing our sons what it means to lead and to love authentically. It's a heavy responsibility, but it's also the greatest privilege.

"Signed Daddy with love… your 1 fan."

A Call to Fathers: Embrace the Responsibility

Now more than ever, we as fathers must step up to the plate. The world is changing rapidly, and our children are being bombarded with influences from every direction. But the most important influence in their lives is us. We have the power to shape their futures, to give them the tools they need to succeed, and to provide them with the love and support they need to thrive.

It's not enough to just be present now we have to be intentional. We have to challenge ourselves to grow in areas of emotional intelligence and maturity. We have to be the fathers our children need us to be. Whether it's teaching our daughters how to navigate the world with confidence and grace or showing our sons what it means to be strong, compassionate men, our role is crucial.

We are the foundation. We are the blueprint. And the legacy we leave behind will shape the future for generations to come.

How You Can Change Your Algorithm

Here are a few steps you can take to change your algorithm and improve the way you show up as a father or role model:

1. **Embrace Emotional Intelligence**

    Take time to listen to your children. Create an environment where they feel safe to be vulnerable and to express their true selves without fear of judgment.

2. **Model the Behavior You Want to See**

    Children learn by watching how you move in the world. Be intentional about the example you set. Demonstrate love, respect, patience, and discipline in your everyday life, and they will follow your lead.

3. **Nurture Their Growth**

    Guide them without imposing your expectations on who they should become. Allow them the space to grow into their own identity while giving them the tools and values they need to navigate life successfully.

CHAPTER SIX

HoodGeek

"We don't have to choose between where we come from and our intellect. Embrace your genius!"

I spent the first few years of school attending JC Napier Elementary in south Nashville. What is apparent now is how I was immersed in an environment that shaped how I saw the world and myself. By the time I got to Maplewood High School, I began to realize just how much my surroundings were influencing me. Back in 5th and 6th grade, I had been part of a gifted program designed to prepare students to go a Magnet school and eventually Vanderbilt. But none of my close friends were in that program, and I was fighting a pull to be in a different crowd. Fast forward to Maplewood High School and being in honors classes just wasn't something that was embraced.

That's where the concept of HoodGeek was born. HoodGeek isn't just a brand, it's an identity that resonates with those that want to embrace everything that makes them who they are. Society often tries to define us by our circumstances, telling us that our environment limits who we can become. But HoodGeek is about reclaiming that narrative. It's about embracing where we come from while recognizing the genius that lies within us. We don't have to pick between where we come from and pursuing intellectual growth. HoodGeek is about tapping into that brilliance, pushing past the stereotypes, and showing the world that our genius isn't limited by our surroundings it is fueled by them.

Embrace Your Past, Embrace Your Struggles

Growing up in the inner city of Nashville, we didn't even realize how deeply we had normalized struggle. It wasn't something we questioned because it was just life as we knew it. As kids, we were already being programmed by what we saw and heard. Survival behaviors were passed down and embedded in our way of living before we even understood what was happening. Whether it was the violence in the streets, the lack of resources, or the systemic barriers that came with being born into certain circumstances, those experiences shaped us. But at the time, it all felt normal. We didn't recognize the trauma because it was all we knew.

"It's time to wake up the culture, too much trauma, hope it finally change."

These lyrics speak to that universal truth: trauma becomes part of your story, even before you realize it. We grow up adapting to environments that push us to survive, but rarely thrive. The truth is, these early experiences set the stage for our lives long before we fully understand their impact. But the important realization is that while the trauma is real, we don't have to be stuck in it. Change doesn't come from waiting on the world to shift for us; it starts from within. We have the power to break these cycles, to rewrite the script that was handed to us, and transform those early survival instincts into something greater, something that builds the future we deserve.

"All our prodigies doing 20 years, no Bronny James."

Imagine feeling like you were growing up with Bronny James, except there was no LeBron to set the stage, no guidance to keep them on the right track, and no real opportunity to fulfill the promises they had. That was the reality for a lot of people I grew up with, some of them even close friends. These were the guys everyone knew had the talent, the ones who could've gone to the NBA or made it big in football. But the truth is, without someone to help guide that talent, many of our dreams die in a prison cell.

Before we made it to high school, so many of those same people were already caught up in the streets, in prison, or battling addiction. Not because they weren't capable of greatness, but because the environment we came from wasn't built to let them shine. It wasn't designed to help us reach our potential—it was designed to keep us locked into survival mode.

I was fortunate to have a mother who provided structure, discipline, and a constant reminder that I was capable of more. She gave me the foundation a lot of others didn't have. For every one of us who managed to break through, there were ten more that fell victim to the traps that were set.. That experience opened my eyes to how critical it is to have someone who reinforces the belief that there's more out there, that you don't have to settle for the life in front of you. Without that, it's easy to lose sight of what's possible and get trapped in a cycle you don't even know how to escape.

So many of us were just trying to survive. We grew up in environments that didn't nurture growth or celebrate brilliance; they were places where getting by day-to-day was the focus. A lot of kids never had a chance to realize their potential because their surroundings didn't offer any paths forward.

But I've also seen the other side and witnessed the few who manage to rise above the circumstances, who break the cycle, and defy the expectations placed on them.

That's the reality for so many of us we're either swept up or fighting to stand out, and the difference often comes down to who was able to see something bigger for themselves in the middle of it all.

Looking back, I realize that the very people we called "nerds" in school are often the ones who go on to build companies, become employers, and create opportunities. These are the people who understood, early on, the power of knowledge and how far it could take them. Meanwhile, many of us were so focused on fitting in that we didn't realize the ones who stood out were the ones building futures for themselves. It's wild to think that the people we once teased are now the ones shaping industries and making the decisions that impact the world.

If there's one thing, I wish I could tell kids today, it's that embracing your intelligence is one of the most powerful things you can do. Being smart is not something to downplay t's something to really embrace. Too many of us are afraid to stand out for the right reasons. We'd rather blend in than shine for what makes us special. Life has shown me that embracing your intelligence is the first step toward breaking down the barriers that try to keep us boxed in. You don't have to follow the crowd. Intelligence is what opens doors, creates opportunities, and puts you in control of your own future.

Embrace Your Genius

"Embrace your fam, embrace your teams, embrace your scars, embrace your genius."

Now more than ever, kids are imitating a lifestyle many people only pretend to live. The rappers they look up to often have stable lives—families, even marriages—while their music sells a reality of chaos, addiction, and recklessness. They're promoting a culture that's just a mask, and for young people who crave acceptance, this can create a real sense of dissonance. They're pulled between what they see online and what they feel inside, leading to an internal struggle over who they're supposed to be.

This is the heart of HoodGeek: embracing everything that makes you, *you*. Embrace your family, even if they're not perfect. Embrace your team, your community, the people who've stood by you. Embrace your scars because they tell the story of your resilience. And most importantly, embrace your genius no whatever form it takes.

But here's the challenge: too many of us don't even realize we have that genius inside. Society has defined "genius" with such a narrow lens that we start believing we don't fit it. I've come to see that every person has a gift that can impact the world. I've seen street hustlers with the strategic minds to run major companies, people who've been overlooked simply because they didn't fit the mold. Too often, that genius gets trapped because no one ever told them their skills were bigger than their environment.

HoodGeek is about breaking those limits and showing the next generation that they don't need to conform to a false narrative. Real power, real success, comes from embracing who you are and realizing that the value you bring isn't in trying to fit in but standing out.

"I walked straight up out the booth and now I'm in a corporate office adjacent to people that doubted my placement."

They didn't recognize my genius because they couldn't see it through the lens I came from. But the same brilliance that helped me navigate the streets is what's driving my success in business today. The difference isn't in the talent—it's in how you use it. It all starts with owning it. Once you recognize your own greatness, no one can take that from you.

Born With Genius, Just Need Exposure

Every one of us is born with a genius and special gift. But the problem is that too many of us don't see ourselves in certain things because we lack exposure. How can you aspire to be a coder, an engineer, or an entrepreneur if you've never been shown those possibilities?

One of the biggest lessons I've learned is that you can't be what you don't see. We need representation, but more importantly, we need exposure. If we don't expose our kids to opportunities, how will they ever know that their genius isn't limited to sports, music, or hustling? If they don't see Black doctors, tech leaders, or business owners, how can they envision themselves in those roles?

Imagine a world where Black kids aren't just consumers of the future, but the ones building it. The power in that shift would be undeniable—a ripple effect of empowerment that transforms entire generations. When we teach our kids to be creators—whether in tech, business, or life—they stop waiting for permission. They stop accepting the narrative society hands them and start designing their own path, becoming the architects of their own destiny.

We have to break free from the role of just being consumers. Too often, we're sold dreams but never taught how to create them. But imagine if we flipped that narrative—if we became the ones building instead of just buying. The power of creation is revolutionary. It shifts your entire perspective. You stop accepting what's handed to you and start shaping the world on your own terms. It's no longer about settling for what's offered; it's about making what you envision a reality.

The Importance of Representation

"HoodGeek the movement, it's important to paint pictures."

Representation is everything. I remember attending AfroTech in Austin and feeling the energy of over 10,000 Black professionals in tech, all focused on building and innovating. It wasn't just inspiring—it was a powerful reminder of the shifts we're creating. Seeing Black entrepreneurs owning restaurant chains, retail stores, and leading industries showed me how far we've come from just being consumers—we're becoming creators of culture and business.

Even more impactful is seeing Black educators and policymakers stepping up, ensuring that our education systems and laws are designed with us in mind. These are the people shaping a future where we don't just participate—we lead, and we create lasting change for the generations coming behind us. This is what empowerment looks like when we take control of our narrative.

"G had 600 black doctors in Manhattan out buying sections."

Flying to New York and walking into a room filled with over 500 Black physicians was a moment that shook me in the best way possible. It was powerful—a reminder that we've got a whole community of change agents, people who are literally healing and saving lives, who are out here making this happen. It's one thing to hear about Black excellence, but to *see* it, to be surrounded by it, was a different level. These are the moments that give you the energy that keeps pushing you forward.

We need these reminders because too often, we get stuck thinking that success looks like one thing—it's something we've got to fight extra hard to achieve because of where we come from or what we've been told. But the reality is, we are redefining that narrative every single day. We belong in every space, we're thriving in fields that weren't designed with us in mind, and we're creating our own platforms when the doors are closed. This is the energy that fuels not just the individual, but the whole community.

Representation isn't just about breaking into industries; it's about changing the narrative for future generations. When young Black kids see doctors, engineers, and CEOs who look like them, it expands their sense of what's possible. It gives them permission to dream beyond the limitations society tries to place on them. It's a ripple effect—once one of us makes it, we open the door for the next.

Embrace What Makes You, You

One of the most powerful messages in HoodGeek is the idea of embracing every part of who you are.

"Stay in them books, it's time to make it cool / And calculate your moves, always embrace the things that make you, you."

I made the decision to dedicate more time to speaking about HoodGeek at schools and youth events because I believe we need to be on the ground floor, doing the real work. We can't just sit back and talk about the problems. We have to show these kids the value of education, knowledge, and the power that comes from using their intellect. It's not enough to tell them they need to *see* it. They need to understand that being smart, strategic, and informed is the real key to success. That's why I've chosen to step into these spaces and be a visible example of what's possible.

One of my favorite poems is Man in the Arena, because it speaks to those who are in the trenches, who are doing the work not just talking about it from the sidelines. That's the energy we need to bring to these kids. We've got to make them see that their brains are their greatest asset. The streets might teach survival, but intellect and knowledge are what will take them to the next level. It's time we make being smart the new standard. The more we show up, the more they'll realize that their differences are what will make them thrive.

We have to show the youth the power of owning every part of who they are. We're not here to fit into molds that weren't made for us. We're here to break them, to redefine success, and to show that genius can come from anywhere.

The Movement of HoodGeek

"I don't want no credit; I don't want shine / I want my people to be aligned."

This is bigger than individual success. It's about collective progress. It's about seeing all of us rise, about creating opportunities for the next generation to excel in ways we never thought possible.

We're in a time where it's more important than ever to be aligned—to be focused on what really matters and to support each other in reaching new heights. The HoodGeek mentality isn't just about personal growth; it's about building communities that thrive together. It's about making sure that the kids who come from the same places we did have the tools and the confidence to pursue their dreams.

Final Thoughts: Embrace Your Genius

At the heart of everything is this truth: embracing who you are, fully and unapologetically, is your greatest power. Your upbringing, your family, your struggles, and your intelligence—they're all part of the blueprint that shapes you. The moment you start embracing all of it, you shift the entire trajectory of your life.

The algorithm society feeds us glorifies the wrong things—surface-level success, materialism, and comparison. It wants us to chase what's shiny, but shallow, pushing us further from who we truly are. But switching the algorithm means choosing to reject that limited version of success. It's about reclaiming control over your life, shifting your focus, and deciding to live with purpose instead of being distracted by illusion. When you change what you pay attention to, you change what influences you, and that changes your whole reality.

You don't have to conform to anyone else's blueprint for success. You don't have to downplay your intelligence or deny where you come from. You can embody both—coming from the streets and carrying the brilliance to change your world. That's what HoodGeek is all about: rewriting the narrative, breaking the mold, and showing the world that success isn't one-dimensional it's as complex and dynamic as you are.

Every single one of us is born with a genius, a spark that has the potential to transform our lives. Too many of us are never told that we carry this power within us. But if we're going to switch the algorithm, we have to start by recognizing our own brilliance. By embracing that, we shatter barriers, redefine success on our terms, and show the world that we're more than what they expect. We're here to build, to thrive, and to lead the way forward. This is what it means to switch the algorithm.

How You Can Change Your Algorithm:

1. **Embrace Your Genius**

    Understand that you have a unique gift inside you. Invest in your growth by seeking knowledge, skills, and mentorship to help you elevate. When you embrace your genius, you begin to unlock your full potential.

2. **Define Success for Yourself**

    Stop chasing what society says success should look like. Decide what your vision of success is—whether it's in business, community leadership, or personal growth—and focus on achieving it.

3. **Stay Grounded**

    Your background gives you a unique edge. Don't feel the need to fit a mold or hide your story—use it to fuel your ambition. Surround yourself with people who support your growth.

HoodGeek

(2)

(3)

HoodGeek

(4)

CHAPTER SEVEN

The Goal is the Goal

"Feelings change, but commitment is non-negotiable, because when the motivation fades, the goal is still the goal."

Link to Song: The Goal is The Goal

The Goal is the Goal

When it comes to reaching anything meaningful in life, one truth stands out: the goal is the goal. Once you set it, the only thing left is commitment by sticking to it no matter what. But here's the real question: why do so many people start with all this energy only to fall off as soon as things get tough?

Think about something as simple as a car wash subscription. Why would a company offer unlimited $20 washes for $39 a month? Because they know most people sign up, get a couple of washes, then start coming less often or forget they even have the membership altogether. It's no accident; the business relies on human nature. We're quick to commit when the hype is fresh, but without consistency, that commitment fades fast. I know this because I've been that person, paying for a membership and barely using it.

This isn't just a car wash model but a life model. New goals, resolutions, fresh beginnings, they feel great in the moment. But staying committed? That's where the real work begins. The truth is, most people quit when it stops feeling exciting, and that's where success slips away.

The challenge isn't about setting the goal; it's about sticking with it. Are you willing to keep pushing when the motivation fades? Because if the goal is the goal, then you find a way, no matter what.

"I don't negotiate ... should bet on Pivot if you knew the truth."

If you could've been a fly on the wall during some of those conversations between Josh and me, you'd have seen a different side of the grind. There were days when we'd sit there, staring at numbers, trying to figure out how to make a five-figure payroll work while we were still waiting on deposits that seemed like they'd never come. We didn't have all the answers; sometimes, we barely had any. And those long drives back from out-of-town meetings? They were real-life brainstorm sessions, where we had no choice but to dig into the depths of our creativity, pulling out whatever ideas we could to keep the business alive.

Pivot hitting the five-year mark wasn't just a milestone; it was a testament to grit. There were so many moments where, by any logical measure, we should've folded. I am talking about kind of struggle that makes you question everything, that makes the road ahead look impossible. But here's the thing: we didn't quit because we decided from day one that quitting wasn't an option. We didn't start this journey for convenience or a quick win. We started because the goal was the goal, and once we set it, excuses were off the table.

This is bigger than motivation we are talking about discipline. It's about making a decision so strong that it overrides every setback, every doubt. No matter what we faced, we committed to finding a way through. It's easy to say you're all in when things are smooth, but the real test comes when things get hard. When you make the goal non-negotiable, you move beyond what's convenient and into what's necessary. You stop looking for an exit and start creating ways forward. That's where resilience is built. That's where success becomes inevitable.

Here's the hard truth: most people won't make it because they lose focus when it gets tough. But if you're one of the few who can push through the discomfort, who can keep grinding when others fall off, you'll separate yourself from the pack. The world rewards those who don't flinch under pressure. So set your goal, lock in, and make it non-negotiable. Because once you've decided, the Goal is the Goal!

Commitment is Non-Negotiable

When you decide on your goals, you're not just saying, "I want this." You're making a pact with yourself. You're saying, "I will do whatever it takes to achieve this." And once you've made that decision, everything else falls into place. Distractions don't matter. Obstacles don't matter. People's opinions don't matter. The only thing that matters is the goal.

"Plenty of people making noise but ain't making plans."

These lyrics hit hard because I see it all the time—people more concerned with *looking* successful than actually being successful. They're caught up in appearances, investing energy into the image of success rather than the real grind that brings it. I used to say, "Lie to me, but don't lie to yourself," because the real issue is that many are fooling themselves about what they truly want or are willing to do. They've become what they think people expect them to be, living in a constant state of contradiction. This disconnect between what they say they want and what they're actually doing is what holds them back from real growth.

Everyone loves to share their dreams, but when you look closer, it's clear most haven't made any real moves. They're making noise, but they're stuck in place, failing to put in the work. If you're truly committed to something, you have to move beyond the talk and start executing.

Your goals can't be something you hype yourself up for and then drop when the excitement fades. Real success requires daily commitment, even when the process gets hard or boring. It's not up for negotiation—it's a decision you make and stand by, no matter what. It's not just about setting the goal, it's about being locked in, day in and day out, until that goal is met.

Falling in Love with the Process

The biggest shift for me came when I stopped obsessing over the end result and fell in love with the process. We started this challenge at Pivot in 2023 where we committed to doing 300 push-ups a day. It really wasn't even about hitting a number but holding ourselves to a standard of discipline, no matter what. Even though I had days where my chest was hurting or I was feeling pain in my elbows from pushing too hard I remembered, "The goal is the goal." It became a code for pushing each other to stay locked in. This wasn't just about physical reps; it was about the mindset and consistency required to get anywhere in life.

This commitment created a system of accountability that forced us to show up every day, even when we didn't feel like it. Whether we were tired, busy, or stressed we were committed. The goal stayed the goal. This type of routine builds the mental toughness that translates into every other area of your life. You become flexible with the route, but the result stays constant.

Discipline Over Motivation

If you really know me, you might think I run on endless motivation, but the truth is, there are days when that drive just isn't there. That's when you have to fall back on something stronger like systems that keep you moving even when you don't feel like it.

One thing we realized while scaling Pivot was that the true measure of a business isn't just about what happens when you're around; it's about what happens when you're not. Are the systems in place strong enough to run without you? Can they carry the load even when you're not at your best? Are they so clear and efficient that, on your hardest days, the process still runs smoothly?

Motivation comes and goes because it's unpredictable. One day you're ready to conquer everything in front of you, and the next, you're struggling to get out of bed. Discipline is different. Discipline is what keeps you on track when the motivation fades. It's the foundation that pushes you to keep going, even when every part of you wants to stop.

"Highly intellectual with discipline is hard to stop."

We live in a world that glorifies motivation. Everyone's chasing that next burst of energy, that next moment of inspiration. But the reality is, the people who achieve great things aren't relying on motivation—they're relying on discipline. They've built habits that keep them on track, even when they don't feel like it. They've made their goals non-negotiable, and they live by that decision every day, regardless of how motivated they feel.

The key to success isn't being motivated all the time but being disciplined enough to keep going even when you're not. It's about setting routines, making sacrifices, and sticking to the plan, even when things get tough. That's the foundation for creating the life you want.

Block the Excuses

When you commit to your goals, you've got to block out excuses like you're dodging those toll-free spam calls.

"Gotta block excuses like they hit you from a toll-free."

Excuses are like those calls that show up as possible scam relentlessly. But just like you hit decline when you see that toll-free number pop up, you've got to shut down those excuses the minute they creep in.

Excuses will tell you every reason why today isn't the day, why you should hold off, why you're not ready. But in reality, excuses are just lies you use to stay comfortable. And comfort? It's a dream killer. Growth only happens when you're willing to push past the easy route, past the urge to sit back and coast. So, block out the noise, block out the excuses, and stay focused on the grind.

I've seen it play out so many times where people fail not because they can't do it but because they let their excuses win. They'll have a laundry list of reasons why things didn't go as planned, but all those reasons? Just roadblocks they put up to protect themselves from feeling like they failed. But failure's not something you dodge it is how you grow. You keep moving forward, learning from every stumble. The only thing standing between you and your goals is the excuse you're still making.

Big Dreams, Bigger Plans

"Big dreams, it ain't ever really what it seems / Subconscious intervenes but it's behind the scenes."

We all start off with big dreams. At some point, every one of us imagined something huge for ourselves. But here's the truth: it's not failure that kills those dreams it is fear of failing. A lot of people decide it's better to not try at all because if they don't try, they can't fail. It's like we convince ourselves that staying small is somehow safer. That mindset is the real dream killer. Life, parents, and our own limiting beliefs slowly chip away at our ambitions until we start shrinking our dreams just to fit into a box that feels less risky.

The Goal is the Goal

Dreams are just the starting point, like a car sitting in the driveway with no gas. It might look good, but it's not going anywhere until you fuel it with action. And that's where most people get stuck because they love the idea of success, but they never take the steps to make it happen. It's not enough to say, "I want to be successful" or "I want to start a business." What does that actually mean? What's the game plan? What are you doing tomorrow to move closer to it? Dreams without a plan are just wishful thinking.

We live in a world where it's easy to talk a big game, to make it look like you're active just because you posted something on Instagram. But here's the real question: are you willing to do what it takes when no one's watching? Are you ready to make sacrifices and push through discomfort? Because talking about your dreams won't make them happen. You have to take risks, put in the hours, and keep going even when it's hard. A lot of times people aren't willing to take that leap and stay where it's safe and comfortable. The reality that's the graveyard for all things great.

No Distractions, No Detours

Once you set your goal, it's time to cut out the noise. Everything else becomes secondary.

If you're serious about your goal, distractions can't be part of the equation. It's not just about saying you want something it's about making sure everything you do aligns with that.

"I talk about it, orchestrate it, then I implement it."

Execution matters more than ideas. You've got to move beyond just talking about what you're going to do and start executing. Learn to say no to anything that doesn't push you closer to your goal. It's not selfish t's necessary. People who succeed aren't just disciplined in their work; they're disciplined in their focus.

I've learned that routines are powerful whether we realize it or not, we all have them. The problem is, many of our routines work against us. They reinforce negative thinking, bad habits, and self-imposed limits.

That's why you need to *build a routine that makes success inevitable*. It's not about doing the work only when you're inspired but showing up every day, no matter how you feel. Routines shape your life, and if you let them, they can either push you forward or hold you back. Think about the habits you're repeating daily without even realizing it. Are they pushing you toward your goals, or are they keeping you stuck?

Block out time and make it non-negotiable. It's easy to underestimate the power of small actions repeated over time, but consistency is what separates people who talk from people who make things happen.

Success isn't about doing something huge all at once but making sure your daily habits align with the future you're trying to create.

And remember, always keep your *why* in front of you. Why are you doing this? Is it for your family? For your future? For something bigger than yourself? When the grind gets tough, and it will, that's what keeps you going. When you're locked in on your purpose, *setbacks become speed bumps, not roadblocks*. When the goal is non-negotiable, *you push forward no matter what*.

Final Thoughts: Commit and Execute

The foundation of creating the life you want is making committed, unwavering decisions. The goal is the goal, and once you've set it, there's no room for negotiation. There's no space for hesitation. It's about locking in on what you want and doing whatever it takes to make it happen. That means building discipline, blocking excuses, and taking action day after day, no matter what.

In the end, success isn't about who's the loudest or who's got the biggest dreams. It's about who's willing to commit, who's willing to make the sacrifices, and who's willing to do the work, consistently, over time. The goal is the goal. Make it non-negotiable and watch how everything else falls into place.

Your dreams are valid. Your goals are achievable. But the difference between wanting something and having it is the commitment you make to yourself. So, set the goal, lock in, and don't stop until you get there.

How You Can Change Your Algorithm

1. **Set One Focused Goal**

   Instead of juggling multiple goals at once, narrow your focus to one major goal that will have the biggest impact on your life. When your energy is spread too thin, it's easy to get distracted. Choose the goal that truly matters and direct your full attention towards it.

2. **Winning Environment**

   Your environment plays a huge role in your success. If you're surrounded by distractions, negativity, or people who don't support your growth, it's going to be harder to reach your goal. Create an environment—whether physical or mental—that sets you up to win.

3. **Consistency Over Intensity**

   It's easy to burn out when you start too fast or go too hard. Focus on small, consistent steps rather than massive, unsustainable actions.

CHAPTER EIGHT

It's a Trend

"Anyone can do it once, but can you do it again? Consistency is where real change happens and where success is built."

Link to Song: It's a Trend

One day, someone approached me, saying, "Q, I really want to do what you're doing. What do I need to do?" I looked at him and said, "I can give you the game plan, but it goes back over 10 years." He seemed a little taken aback, so I explained further, "If you're willing to put in the work, you can definitely get there in 5 years." His response? "Five years? That's way too long." I had to remind him that the time will pass anyway. In five years, you can either be where you want to be, or still talking about what where you want to go.

Success isn't about hitting a high point once; it's about showing up, day in and day out, until it becomes part of who you are. It's easy to get drawn in by the idea of being a trending topic, to chase that moment in the spotlight. But trends are temporary. The real question is: can you do it again? Can you build something that lasts, something you can keep growing and evolving? That's where the real success lies.

It's a Trend is about understanding that consistency is the real key to lasting success. It's not enough to just do something once. The people who make it, the ones who really leave their mark, are the ones who can repeat that success over and over, until it becomes a pattern in their life. That's the kind of energy I'm talking about in this chapter. My question is always can you go do it again?

The Power of Repetition

"Yeah again and again I tell them go do it again / Yeah again and again I do it again and again."

Steve Jobs mastered the art of consistency with the iPhone, building trust through repetition until it was the default choice. Each year, Apple didn't just release a phone—they reinforced an experience, a vision, so that over time, we stopped comparing it to other brands. We just knew. Reflecting on that, I see how this same principle has played out in my own journey. When I consistently show up, refining what I create, people start to trust the vision without needing to question it. It's a powerful reminder that real impact isn't about one big moment but showing up again and again, until what you're building speaks for itself.

Consistency is what makes people trust you. Whether it's your business, your relationships, or your personal growth. You've got to build a reputation for being reliable, for showing up and delivering, even when the excitement fades. That's what builds a solid foundation. That's what turns fleeting success into lasting impact.

Falling in Love with the Process

"I ain't putting diamonds in watches, ain't busting down nothing but doors / When you in love with the process, you don't even look at the score."

I remember when I read *The Compound Effect* by Darren Hardy. He told a story of the magic penny and how it is doubling it every day for 31 days turns into over $10 million. That example shifted my entire perspective on where real success happens. It's not in the big wins but in the small, consistent actions taken over time.

That idea of compounding effort reminds me of the Chinese bamboo tree. For years, you water it, nurture it, and see nothing happening above ground. You're putting in work, but to anyone watching, it looks like nothing's changing. You've got to trust the process, believe that all that unseen work is building something solid. Then, suddenly, in a matter of weeks, it grows 90 feet into the air. Those years of hidden effort are what make the rapid growth possible. Success works the same way because the foundation is built long before anyone sees the results. It's a reminder that every day you show up, you're setting the stage for something bigger than you can see right now.

When we fall in love with the process, we stop obsessing over the results. We don't check the scoreboard every minute because we trust that putting in the work will eventually bring the rewards. Sometimes we get consumed by the outcome, craving the win, the payday, the recognition. But the people who truly succeed are the ones focused on the bigger picture, understanding that the rewards come naturally when they commit to the journey. If we're in it for the process, whether it's building a business, creating art, or mastering a skill we've already won. The results are just a byproduct of that dedication to the grind.

Consistency Is a Trend

"If you ain't ever consistent then tell me bro how would you know."

Here's the thing: a lot of people cut themselves short before they've even truly begun. They can list all the reasons something won't work, but those reasons are often just fears disguised as logic. They plan for failure before they've even taken the first real step, minimizing their potential because they've never given success the consistency it requires. The truth is, many people never see what they could achieve because they stop showing up when it matters most.

Consistency is like training your subconscious to run on a program aligned with your goals. Every day you show up, putting in the work, you're reinforcing a mindset that naturally pushes you closer to what you want. Repetition rewires you to no longer see challenges as barriers, but as part of the journey that strengthens your resolve.

This steady dedication shapes your thoughts, making progress feel less like a daily struggle and more like second nature. It's like creating an autopilot for success, where even when you're not consciously thinking about it, you're moving forward. The small steps, repeated consistently, shift your entire perspective. It's in these moments that your mindset transforms, your resilience grows, and every step feels like it's bringing you closer to your vision.

The Trend of Repeated Success

We follow so many trends today. From fashion to social media, to the latest viral challenges, it's easy to jump on whatever's hot in the moment. But one trend that we need to lock into is the power of repeated success. Repeated effort. Repeated commitment. Too many people focus on doing something once, and they think they've made it. But the real question is: can you do it again? And again? And again?

It's not just about achieving success once; it's about making success a habit. It's about showing up every day and putting in the work, regardless of how you feel. It's about building momentum through repetition. When you can make success a trend in your life, that's when you've truly arrived.

We talk so much about reciprocal energy and wanting the same effort and commitment from others that we give out. But here's the truth: have you been consistent? Have you done it again and again? Too many of us want the rewards without putting in the sustained effort. If you want to be successful in any area you've got to put in the work repeatedly.

So many people are looking to become entrepreneurs. So many people want to get married and build strong families. But the answer to maintaining those commitments is hidden in the power of repetition. It's about doing the work over and over, even when it gets tough, even when it's not exciting anymore. That's how you build something that lasts.

It's a Trend

Building Brick by Brick

"I'm gone build it up brick after brick."

It's not about making a huge leap forward all at once. it's about steady, consistent progress. Building brick by brick may not be the dopamine rush we desire, but it's how real success is built. Each brick represents a small step forward, a piece of the foundation that supports everything you're working toward.

The constant need for instant results is killing our ability to collaborate, to work with synergy, and to build something lasting. We're addicted to the idea that success, happiness, or fulfillment should come immediately. This mindset isn't just making us anxious; it's driving a lot of us to medication.

We've been conditioned by the algorithm to think everything should happen instantly. The lack of patience isn't just an inconvenience but a self-inflicted wound that's widening the gap between where we are and where we could be. We're losing out on synergy because we're too busy trying to "make it" overnight. But anything worth building, especially in our community, takes time, effort, and a collective mindset that values long-term vision over instant gratification. When you constantly chase quick highs, you miss out on the deeper, more meaningful connections that come from the slow burn of collaboration.

The truth is, this instant craving is the reason we're struggling. It's why so many of us are burnt out, frustrated, and feeling like we're not enough. But we have to understand that success isn't a sprint, it's a marathon. Until we embrace that, we'll keep running in circles, trying to medicate the very anxiety we're creating.

Final Thoughts: Make Success a Trend

In the end, success isn't about one big moment. It's about building a trend of repeated success in your life. It's about showing up, putting in the work, and doing it again and again until it becomes second nature. When you can do that, success isn't just something you achieve—it's who you are.

The challenge is simple: focus on consistency. Fall in love with the process. Block out the noise, stay focused on your path, and commit to building brick by brick. If you can do that, success won't just be a moment—it'll be a trend. And that's what will set you apart from everyone else.

How You Can Change Your Algorithm?

1. Redefine Success in Real Terms

   Shift your focus from the end result to the value of daily progress. Instead of measuring success by how fast you can achieve something, start measuring it by how well you show up each day.

2. Control Your Inputs

   What you consume influences how you think. If what you're feeding your mind is all about instant results and comparison, you'll feel that pressure. Instead, curate your inputs to align with the mindset of patience, growth, and sustainable success.

3. Master the Art of Course Correction

   Life doesn't follow a straight path, and neither does success. Don't be afraid to adjust your approach as you move forward. Set your goal, yes, but remain flexible in how you get there. Understand that detours and setbacks aren't failures—they're part of the process.

It's a Trend

CHAPTER NINE

Designer Habits

"It's time to shift from consumers to creators and redefine how we determine our value."

Link to Song: Designer Habits

"Got designer habits, expensive fabrics / Come to fashion, she just gotta have it."

Fashion has always been deeply intertwined with Black culture. We utilized our clothing as more than just a way to look good but a symbol of identity and a powerful means of signaling success. For as long as I can remember fashion has been our way of expressing resilience, creativity, and the belief that regardless of the challenges we face, we have the ability to rise above and define ourselves on our own terms. I still remember being in high school, standing in line with my stepdad Kenny at *Just for Feet* at midnight, all so I could be the first to walk into school wearing the new Jordans the next day. In college I remember so many people spending their entire student loan refund checks on clothes.

The real issue arises when we allow designer brands to dictate our identity, when we let the logos, we wear determine our sense of worth. *Designer Habits* is about waking up to the fact that our obsession with showcasing success is the very thing preventing us from truly achieving it. If we can shift our mindset from short-term validation to long-term legacy, we'll stop just imitating wealth and start creating it. It's time to harness our collective power, redefine our values, and invest in the future we talk about, rather than simply dressing the part.

"Love the attention, she attracts, that shit automatic / She already got her caption, update her status."

We live in a time where the dopamine rush from social validation has become addictive. Every new purchase, every status update, every photo comes with that brief high from the likes, the comments, and the feeling that you're being seen. It's a quick hit of confidence, a moment where you feel elevated because the world is watching. But here's the thing: most of the people you think care don't actually care as much as you think. They'll scroll past your post and move on to the next, and you're left chasing another high, another moment of validation.

The reality is there is nothing wrong with wanting or enjoying the nice things in life. When you work hard, you should celebrate your wins and treat yourself to whatever makes you feel good. The problem isn't in the desire for nice things; it's in letting that desire dominate your mindset, cloud your goals, and ultimately, distract you from what really matters.

We've become so obsessed with looking successful that we sometimes lose track of *being* successful. There's a fine line between celebrating your progress and becoming consumed by the image you're projecting. It's easy to spend money to maintain a facade, but what happens when the attention fades? Are you any closer to your goals, or did you just feed into the cycle of seeking validation from others?

Enjoy the rewards of your grind, but don't let them run your life. It's about more than just what you show the world; it's about the substance behind it. True success comes from staying aligned with your path, not just looking like you've made it.

The Roots of Designer Habits

"Definitely gone feel the image, even if it's tripping / Cameras on, oh they gone see us when we winning".

We live in a world where perception is everything. The way people see us can sometimes feel more important than who we actually are. And it's not just about how we look to others; it's about how we see ourselves through their eyes. That's the power and danger of "designer habits" because they give us an image to uphold, even if that image doesn't match our reality.

Back in the day, commercials were designed to sell us dreams and lifestyles we were told to aspire to. These ads created a hunger for something more, pushing us to chase a vision of success that wasn't even ours. Fast forward to today, and we're bombarded with these "commercials" non-stop, not just from big companies but from influencers who curate lives of luxury, vacations, rented cars with stacks of fake money. And their goal? To keep you feeling like you're behind, like you're missing out if you're not buying into the same illusion.

Here's the thing: a lot of it isn't real. The cars are leased, the lifestyle is borrowed, and the image is just that—an image. But even when we know it's fake, we still fall into the trap. We start feeling like we need to spend more, buy more, just to feel like we belong. That's how we get trapped in this cycle of "designer habits," letting material things define our worth.

We need to switch the mindset from being consumers to creators. There's so much power in that shift. Black-owned brands don't always get the same attention, but they're out here, doing amazing things. That's why I often rock 'HoodGeek'. At some point, you realize *you* are the brand. It's not about keeping up with anyone else's vision of success; it's about building your own. We have to stop chasing the illusion and start recognizing that real value comes from what we build, not from what we buy.

The Price We Pay

"I told her we don't need no Gucci, truthfully you know I'm more Jeezy."

When we get caught up in chasing trends, we often lose sight of what really matters. We start prioritizing things that, in the grand scheme of life, don't hold much value. We become more concerned with appearances than with substance. And that's where things can get dangerous.

Financially, "designer habits" can put us in a tough spot. It's not uncommon to see people spending money they don't have, going into debt, or sacrificing their long-term financial security just to keep up appearances. We justify it by telling ourselves that we'll make it back or that we deserve to benefit from all of our hard work. And while there's truth in rewarding yourself, it becomes problematic when the reward turns into a habit that's financially unsustainable.

Emotionally, the cost can be even higher. When your identity is tied to the things you own, what happens when those things are taken away? The need to always remain at the forefront the latest trend can leave you feeling empty, always needing to buy more just to keep feeling good about yourself.

"Without the latest, still they favorite coach / So how you gone repeat it?"

The reality is that you don't need the latest to validate your worth. Your value isn't tied to a designer label, or any of the stuff we chase to keep up appearances. Strip all that away, and the real question is: would you still know who you are? Would you still walk with the same confidence?

Confidence Comes from Within

The trap with "designer habits" is the belief that confidence comes from what we own or wear. This way of thinking leads to habits like constantly shopping to stay on trend, feeling insecure without the latest look, or spending just to keep up appearances. But real confidence doesn't come from outside approval but from knowing yourself, owning your strengths, and investing in growth. True confidence is built by habits that strengthen your identity, not by anything you could buy.

"See it's in you if it's in you, can't go buy it, gotta be it."

For decades, companies have mastered the art of tying our self-worth to what we wear and own, using psychological tricks designed to tap into our emotions. These weren't just lucky guesses; they used real psychological studies to figure out how to make us believe that without the latest designer, we're somehow lacking. The ads aren't just pushing products; they're pushing an idea, planting the notion that your value is tied to material things.

Let's call it what it is; capitalist mind manipulation. We've been conditioned to think that we're behind in life if we're able to spend relentlessly. It's intentional, and it's been embedded in our culture for years, creating a loop where we're chasing validation through what we buy. The subtle messages are always there.

But real confidence? It comes from within. It's not something you can buy, fake, or flex. We can purchase a closet full of Gucci, but if you don't believe in yourself, none of it matters. When you get that, you stop chasing trends and start building a life based on your own values.

The moment you recognize that your value isn't tied to your wardrobe, everything changes. You move with intention, you stop living for validation from what you can wear, post, or buy. That's when the shift happens, from consumer to creator, from follower to leader. You stop chasing the labels that tell you who you are and start designing your own narrative, building something that can't be measured by material possessions. You realize that the power isn't in the brands you wear—it's in the brand you are, the legacy you're building, and the value you bring to the table.

Switching the Algorithm of Success

We need to shift how we view success and status in our communities. The truth is Black culture has always defined what's cool. We are the trendsetters, the tastemakers. We've been setting the standard for style, music, and culture for generations, but the difference now is we've become heavy consumers rather than creators. Imagine if we switched the algorithm. Instead of simply buying into brands that don't reflect or reinvest into our communities, what if we took the power of the Black dollar and directed it toward Black-owned brands?

There are Black-owned brands that are making waves, but they don't get the full benefit of our trillion-dollar spending power. We have the opportunity to redefine what luxury means by supporting businesses that reinvest in us, that understand our culture, and that value our contributions. We've proven that we have the power to create trends. Now, we need to take control of that narrative and use our influence to uplift our own.

The key is understanding that no amount of money, designer goods, or flashy cars can fill the voids we have inside. The real work is in understanding your value, independent of those things. When you truly know who you are, no matter what you wear, you will exude luxury. You will move with a confidence that cannot be bought because you know your worth.

Becoming Creators

Kanye West is someone who, no matter how you feel about him, can't be ignored when it comes to the blueprint for creation. He's unapologetically always pushing boundaries, always thinking bigger, always making something out of nothing. Kanye didn't just buy into the brands; he became the brand. He showed us that you don't have to just consume what the world gives you, but you can create your own lane, your own empire. And whether you agree with his methods or not, he gave a blueprint that's undeniable: be the creator, not the consumer.

I read a story about a group of guys on a trip, and one of them realized he forgot his Cuban link chain. As soon as he noticed, everything changed and he felt small, out of place, like he wasn't himself. He didn't even want to go out anymore. He stayed in his room, feeling incomplete, and had the chain shipped overnight. The second it arrived, and he put it back on, he said, "I'm back."

This story sums up so much of what's happening right now based on how we tie our identity and confidence to things outside of ourselves. Somewhere along the line, we started believing the facade we were sold: that what you wear, the brand names you flaunt, the chain on your neck determines your worth. We've been conditioned to think that if we don't look a certain way, we're less than. That's a part of what keeps us trapped in the matrix.

We need to teach our kids that the real power isn't in the labels or the chains but their ability to create. Let's show them how to build brands, how to visualize and bring something into existence that didn't exist before. Let's teach them that what really matters and holds real value are things that can't be bought. It's the vision, the creativity, the discipline, and the legacy they build that will make the difference. And once they understand that, they'll stop chasing the symbols of success and start creating success for themselves.

Conclusion: The Real Designer

In the end, we have to ask ourselves: What are we really designing? Are we designing a life that's built on substance, or are we just decorating the surface? Designer habits can be fun, they can be flashy, and they can feel good in the moment. But if they're not grounded in something real, they won't last.

The real designer habit is the habit of investing in yourself, knowing your worth, and creating a life of purpose and substance. Let's start building from the inside out, focusing on what truly matters. The clothes, the cars, the luxury is just extra. The real luxury is knowing your worth and designing a life that reflects it.

How You Can Change Your Algorithm

If you're ready to break free from "Designer Habits" and start building something real, here's how you can shift your mindset:

1. Detach Your Identity from Possessions

   Understand that your value doesn't come from what you own. When you realize your identity is not for sale, you'll start to make decisions that serve your growth, not just your appearance.

2. Prioritize Long-Term Value Over Short-Term Gains

   Instead of spending money on things that only give you momentary satisfaction, invest in things that will elevate your future. This could mean putting money into stocks, real estate, or even self-development programs.

3. Shift from Consumer to Creator

   Every time you feel the pull to buy something for status, ask yourself what you could create instead. The goal is to move from someone who spends to someone who produces. It's not about denying yourself—it's about understanding that real power comes from creation, not consumption.

CHAPTER TEN

Bring the love back

"Life feels more disconnected than ever, but deep down, we're all trying to bring the love back."

Link to Song: Bring the Love Back

Algorithm of Toxicity

We're living in a time where love feels distant. People are more guarded, relationships feel more strained, and everyday conversations are filled with tension. Yet, deep down, we all want the same thing: real connection. We crave love, not just in our relationships, but in how we approach life. But to get there, we need to step away from the toxicity that's become so normal and bring back the light, the positivity, and the joy in our daily interactions.

This isn't just about romance but how we show up for ourselves, for our families, and for our communities. It's about changing the energy we put out, because that energy shapes everything around us. But to do that, we have to understand how powerful the algorithm is in pulling us away from what matters.

The Algorithm: Why It Works So Well

An algorithm is designed to keep feeding you what you engage with the most. The more you interact with something, the more of it you get. It's a feedback loop and an endless cycle feeding us what we click on, what we watch, and what we spend time on. The problem? The algorithm has learned that we're drawn to negativity, drama, and toxicity, and it keeps us stuck in that loop.

"I'm tryna bring the love back, conversations been too toxic"

What's worse is that this same algorithm is shaping our relationships, our thoughts, and even how we approach life. It's feeding us content that keeps us in survival mode, making us believe that being guarded, untrusting, and always on edge is the way to be. But that's not real. That's the algorithm keeping us away from the one thing we really want, love.

Where is the Love?

I remember when family reunions were a thing and being present with the people who mattered was the priority. Somewhere along the way, we traded those moments for the constant grind of achievement. We've been so focused on reaching the next level, on stacking accolades, that we've lost sight of what truly brings joy. Where are the R&B love songs that used to fill the air with good vibes? Where are the slow jams that made you want to hold your partner a little closer?

We need to bring that love back! The love that wasn't about status, likes, or validation. The kind of love that's built on presence, not performance. But to do that, we've got to be willing to unplug from the algorithm that keeps us chasing after things that don't feed our souls.

The Impact on Our Kids

Our kids are growing up in a world that's more disconnected than ever, where relationships are seen through the lens of social media, and love is measured by likes and followers. They're seeing a version of life that's more about appearance than reality. They're not seeing love but nonstop distractions and competition. We've got to ask ourselves, what are we really teaching them?

The truth is, kids don't need more products, more social media exposure, or more distractions. They need more love. They need to see love modeled in the home, between parents, and within the family. They need to feel that connection, that sense of belonging, that can't be bought or performed online. The algorithm is raising our kids to believe that the more they achieve or the more they show off, the more love they'll get. But we need to flip that script and remind them that love is about who you are, not what you have.

The Pursuit

We've all been told that success means constantly leveling up—more money, more recognition, more possessions. But in that pursuit, we often drift away from what really holds value. How many times have we been so focused on grinding that we missed time with family, ignored a call from a loved one, or skipped a gathering, thinking, "I'll catch the next one, business comes first"? For me, one of the greatest blessings has been building a life where family time isn't something I squeeze in—it's part of my schedule. Being able to show up for a PTO meeting or spend an afternoon with my grandmother on a weekday reminds me of what's real. These moments have brought me back to what grounds me and what makes this journey truly worthwhile.

The real question is: what's the cost? Are we willing to keep sacrificing the people we love in exchange for things that won't matter at the end of the day? Where are the family reunions, the moments where we gather just to celebrate each other, to reconnect, to remind ourselves that we're part of something bigger?

The Law of Attraction: Light Attracts Light

The energy you put out is the energy you get back. If we keep feeding into the negativity, the drama, and the toxicity, that's what we're going to keep attracting into our lives. But if we shift and start putting out more love, more light, more positivity we'll start to see that same energy reflected back to us.

The Law of Attraction is simple: what you focus on expands. If you focus on love, you'll attract more love. If you focus on light, you'll see more light. But the problem is, we've been conditioned by the algorithm to focus on everything that's dark. It's time to change that. It's time to bring the love back.

Self-Love: The Truest Form of Discipline

Here's the thing: before we can bring love back into our relationships, we've got to start with ourselves. Self-love isn't about trying to build he "soft life". Self-love is about discipline. It's about showing up for yourself, even when it's hard. It's about making choices that reflect your worth, your values, and your goals.

When you practice real self-love, you start to set higher standards for your life. You stop tolerating things that don't align with your vision. And once you start showing up for yourself in that way, you'll attract people and opportunities that match that energy. That's the power of self-love raises your vibration, and when you operate at a higher frequency, you draw in higher-quality experiences.

Bring Back the Positivity, Bring Back the Love

We've spent too much time in the dark. We've let the algorithm of negativity shape our relationships, our mindset, and our lives. But it doesn't have to stay that way. It's time to bring the love back. It's time to shift the energy, to reconnect with the people who matter, and to start living in a way that reflects the light we want to see in the world.

What would happen if we made love the focus again? If we spent more time being present, more time showing up for the people we care about, more time feeding our minds with positive energy instead of the constant stream of negativity? We'd see a real shift. Not just in our personal lives, but in our communities, in our culture, in everything.

"Where is the love, we all been at war"

It's time to bring that love back. It starts with each of us, with the choices we make every day. It starts with turning off the toxicity and tuning into the frequency of love. It's about bringing the positivity back to our daily lives and refusing to entertain anything that doesn't align with that.

How You Can Change Your Algorithm

1. Cut Out the Noise

   Be intentional about what you allow into your mind because that's what shapes your reality.

2. Reconnect with Your People

   Reconnect with the people who fill you up and make you feel loved. The grind will always be there, but your people won't.

3. Practice Self-Love Through Discipline

   Self-love isn't just about treating yourself; it's about setting boundaries and holding yourself accountable. Discipline is the highest form of love you can give yourself.

Bring the love back

(5)

(6)

CONCLUSION

A Call to Switch the Algorithm

The world we live in is driven by patterns, algorithms if you will. They're the unseen forces that dictate what we see, how we think, and the choices we make. But those algorithms aren't just lines of code in social media platforms; they are the habits, thoughts, and mindsets that define how we move through life. We all have the power to switch these algorithms that keep us locked in a cycle of negativity or complacency. We can replace them with ones that inspire progress, love, and connection.

Throughout this book, we've journeyed through different facets of life, and each chapter represents an opportunity to reflect on the habits and mindsets we've developed. From thinking big and embracing radical change in *Pivotal Thoughts* to reassessing what really matters in *Since Covid*, we've explored how important it is to take control of our personal algorithms.

Since Covid - A Moment to Reevaluate

Since Covid was a chapter that highlighted a global pause where we all had the chance to reassess our priorities. For many of us, the pandemic was a wake-up call. When everything slowed down, we realized that the things we thought were holding us back weren't external at all; they were within us. The lack of direction, discipline, and purpose became evident when we were given all the time in the world, yet still struggled to achieve our goals.

This chapter was about accepting that we no longer live in the pre-Covid world. Things have changed, and there's no going back. Instead of mourning the loss of "normal," we must focus on what we can create moving forward. *Since Covid* was a reminder to break away from the over-saturated, over-stimulated culture and embrace a more disciplined, intentional approach to life.

Pivotal Thoughts - Shifting Your Mindset

In Pivotal Thoughts, we discussed the power of expanding your mindset to create opportunities. This chapter wasn't just about thinking positively but *thinking deliberately* and pushing past the limitations of our environment and our past programming.

The key takeaway was to understand that your thoughts don't just shape your current reality, but they mold your future. We discussed how the subconscious mind can hold us back if we don't reprogram it and start intentionally thinking about what we want, rather than what we fear. *Pivotal Thoughts* is a blueprint for rewiring our brains and setting the foundation for the life we truly want.

Too Many Followers - Becoming a Leader

In *Too Many Followers,* we discussed the pressure to conform. Social media is filled with people following trends, trying to fit into the latest mold. But the truth is, being a follower doesn't lead to fulfillment, it leads to chasing an ever-moving target. We explored the power of influence and how important it is to step away from following others and start creating your own path.

This chapter was not about leadership in the traditional sense. It's about rejecting the pressure to fit in and learning to trust your own voice, your own intuition, and your own vision. Being a leader in your own life is about making decisions that are aligned with your true purpose, not just with what's popular.

50/50 - The Power of Partnership

In 50/50, we talked about the importance of shared effort in building something lasting. Too often, we get caught up in external conversations about who should pay for what, or who should take on more of the burden. But the truth is, success in relationships comes from a shared commitment to growth, love, and understanding.

50/50 reminded us that real relationships aren't about division but balance and reciprocity. The key to success in love and life is finding harmony with your partner, where both of you contribute equally, not just financially, but emotionally and mentally

Girl Dad/MANnerisms - Redefining Masculinity

Girl Dad/MANnerisms, we reflected on the evolving role of fathers, particularly Black fathers, and the importance of emotional intelligence and vulnerability. This chapter wasn't just about raising daughters but also raising sons, and showing them that real strength comes from compassion, empathy, and love.

We discussed how fathers have the power to set the foundation for their children's sense of self-worth and relationships. It's more important than ever for men to step up emotionally, not just financially, and to create an environment where our children feel loved, respected, and empowered.

HoodGeek - Embracing All Sides of Yourself

In *HoodGeek*, we explored the intersection of intellect and street wisdom, the fusion of both book smarts and survival instincts. This chapter was a celebration of our uniqueness and the idea that you don't have to fit into a narrow mold to succeed. Too often, we compartmentalize ourselves, hiding parts of who we are to fit into society's expectations.

HoodGeek was about embracing the fullness of your identity and understanding that your genius isn't confined to traditional avenues. It's in everything you've experienced, from the streets to the boardroom. This chapter encouraged us to own our complexity and to break the algorithm that tells us we can only be one thing at a time.

The Goal is the Goal - Committing to Your Purpose

The Goal is the Goal emphasized the importance of staying committed to your purpose. It's not about getting distracted by trends, setbacks, or what everyone else is doing. It's about setting a clear goal and then being relentless in your pursuit of it.

We introduced the concept of falling in love with the process, not just the end result. Often, we get caught up in the idea of achieving the goal, but the real magic is in the journey. This chapter explored how committing to your goals, holding yourself accountable, and staying disciplined can make the difference between success and failure.

The goal isn't to just hit a target once but developing the discipline and the mindset to keep hitting that target, again and again, no matter what challenges come your way. We introduced the phrase "The Goal is the Goal" as a lifestyle, one that requires you to be flexible in your approach but unwavering in your commitment to the destination.

It's a Trend - The Power of Consistency

In *It's a Trend*, we discussed the importance of repetition and consistency. The chapter emphasized that success isn't just about reaching a high point once, but about repeating that success over and over again until it becomes second nature. This is where many people falter—they may achieve success once but lack the discipline or commitment to keep showing up and putting in the work consistently.

We explored how trends, by their nature, come and go, but true success is found in building habits and systems that last. Too many people get caught up in chasing fleeting moments of success, but what sets those who last apart from the rest is their ability to maintain their efforts day in and day out.

Designer Habits - Redefining Success

In *Designer Habits,* we explored the culture of materialism and the obsession with status symbols. Too often, we tie our self-worth to the clothes we wear, the cars we drive, or the labels we can afford. This chapter was about breaking that cycle and understanding that true success isn't something you can buy but something you build from within.

We discussed how the algorithm of success has been distorted by external validation and social media trends. But the real designer habit we need to cultivate is the habit of investing in ourselves, our minds, and our skills. True confidence comes from knowing your worth, independent of what you own.

Bring the Love Back: Summary

At the core of Bring the Love Back is a call to reconnect with love, positivity, and meaningful relationships. In a world dominated by the algorithm of toxicity and negativity, it's easy to lose sight of the real essence of life. We've become guarded, distracted, and more focused on achieving status than nurturing genuine connections. This chapter reminds us to shift our focus from superficial success to the kind of love and light that fuels real growth.

It's time to reclaim love in all its forms and bring it back to the forefront of our lives, so we can build a future that's rooted in positivity, connection, and growth.

What's Next?

So, what's next after we switch the algorithm? It's time to take everything we've learned and put it into practice. We can't just talk about change, but we have to live it. Each chapter of this book is a piece of the puzzle, a step in the journey toward a life that is defined by purpose, not by trends.

Switching the algorithm means being intentional about what we consume, how we think, and the habits we cultivate. It's about focusing on what truly matters which is our growth, relationships, and contributions to the world.

As we move forward, the challenge is to keep checking in with ourselves. Are we living in alignment with our goals? Are we investing in the things that truly matter? Are we building habits that support our long-term success, not just our short-term satisfaction?

The work isn't easy, but it's necessary. We all have the power to switch the algorithm of our lives, to break free from the patterns that no longer serve us, and to create a life that is rich in purpose, love, and fulfillment.

This is your life. You have the power to make it extraordinary. Switch the algorithm and start writing a new story.

Coach Q

Poem- New Balance by Raegan Paige

Most of us are angry
Most of us are hurting
Most of us are oblivious to what's really going on
Most of us are like the morning dawn
Waiting for someone to come along
To finish writing the lyrics to our song

Most of all we just want to mean the most to each other
And grow with each other
Taking love that we got from one another to give it to the other
That's our balance
And even when it's silent
Our brains keep the noise up
Sometimes too much
Thinking or overthinking
I can't tell, it's a rush
I can't just brush

This off
Because I knew it was you right away
When all my feelings hit me like a tidal wave
Now I always crave
The way you made me feel
Even though I was whole without you, you completed me
That's how I know it was real

Switch The Algorithm

Some of us do find the one
Some of us know where it all begun
Some of us talk without our words
Some of us find peace in the birds
That sing the songs of love and tranquility

Are you my lover or my enemy
Maybe it's not that deep I don't know what's gotten into me

Song Lyrics

Since Covid

Verse 1- Coach Q

Aye since Covid it's hard to comprehend it

We lost connection we obsessed with all of the pretending

Frustration overload got us lacking decency,

Everything is right there if you could match the frequency

Recently... Seem like the therapist making all the bread...

Cause a couple of tik tok reels can't help you get ahead...

challenged my own thinking, readjusted my lens...

Depression like an obsession but at least they bought them a Benz

Lost my marriage then my mind I wish I could make amends

Seem like we in the matrix and faking it is the trend

All CEOs no workers without a dollar to spend

Scared to read my text msg we lost somebody again

Hook- Coach Q

Aye since Covid it done got dark...

Aye Damn baby where do I start

Since Covid seem like people on decline though

It's time to make a shift but just need to try to climb

Verse 2- Coach Q

Now Republicans tryna take a way abortions
and I ain't no mcm since walking outta Nordstrom
Everyone want their portions but can't even see it's poisoned
Blaming everything but we just a product of all our choices
Found out the worst party is wherever Sean Combs at.
We took out all the triple Ps now gotta pay them loans back
Now ozempic really stopping folks from actually moving
False fallacies seem to overrule what facts is proving
Black was the tech when they was lying about diversity,
Now Trump done put the country in a state of an emergency
Ain't no urgency we taking whatever they handing out
Lately my favorite destinations headed to my granny house,
My boys making notes no I'm not talking about another singer
I know that my kids count on me like a couple fingers
What we doing see so many settling
Now you can make a million by teaching some shit you never did

Hook- Coach Q

Aye since Covid it done got dark…
Aye Damn baby where do I start
Since Covid seem like people on decline though
It's time to make a shift but just need to try to climb

Pivotal Thoughts

Verse 1- Coach Q

I feel like we cloning each other, independence is missing

Spouses just swap um out, ain't no patience to fix it

Stimulation like coffee, I swear they ready to risk it

DND if it's positive, never fail they will miss it

Entitlement-Hypertension, accountable it's deficient

Paint it like I'm DaVinci, but own it like my invention

I feel like I've benefited when reading my brother sentence

My mother covered me up with all positive interference

My friends are doctors and lawyers, mixed with hustlers and workers

Made it through the resistance, never out of the purpose

Can't keep going through our creditors to purchase

A Birkin, you dipping your toe in shit in immersed in

Verse 2- Coach Q

I see they stay sleeping, they daydreaming, they hate leaving

Out the house to go create, but gone say that he gate-keeping

I'm just peeping the culture, it's too steady to shift it

Life has shown me with dead weight, it's too heavy to lift it

I'm a student of excellence, borderline perfectionist

Conversational specialist, the one that they investing with

Switch The Algorithm

I'm spending less energy on it if I ain't affecting it,

I suggest you evaluate who you are connected with it,

I route it for the score and they coming to interfere late

My overnight success been literally 20 years straight

I guess the pictures blurry sometimes without the backdrop

Pivot started with two tee shirts and a laptop

Now its international applications to process

But every 5 sit ups you tryna measure the progress

I see Jordan Pooles confused thinking they Chef now

They box you with the rules I teach um never to step down

Too Many Followers

Hook- Coach Q

I see too many followers aye tell me where the leaders at,

(I see too many follower, I see too many followers)

I see too many followers aye tell me where the leaders at,

(I hear the boy is coming back, I'm guessing they been needing that)

So clap for him, Yea clap for him, clap for him, yea clap for him

(I see too many followers, I see too many followers)

clap for him, yea clap for him, clap for him, yea clap for him

Verse 1-

Was so enthused to prove myself, leave my mark on the game

Multifaceted brain their mental ain't ever the same.

My endeavors insane, come watch your perceptions will change,

Intercepted the lanes and pivoted

I been on…. interventions like building my family business

Employing my children, yeah, I been implementing what I mention

Knew he had to come back it's different when he ain't in it

Intensifying desires I been in a new dimension

Diminish it but will mimic while listening to the gimmicks

You got too many followers that's following what you ain't living

Implementing my hobbies at my offices to decompress

Switch The Algorithm

I'm socially so opposed to posing when he get dressed
I'd be impressed if your jewelry's less than what you invest
I interject a little less now I just choose peace
Would love for you to get baby but I choose me
No need for these long conversations it ain't too deep
I'm too keen on the properties that influence sheep,
No truancy, my attendance in that 2 seat
With my daughter about to go see the lakers
Won't see no motion with shit if you don't go take it

Hook- Coach Q

I see too many followers aye tell me where the leaders at,
(I see too many followers, I see too many followers)
I see too many followers aye tell me where the leaders at,
(I hear the boy is coming back, I'm guessing they been needing that)
So clap for him, Yea clap for him, clap for him, yea clap for him
(I see too many followers, I see too many followers)
clap for him, yea clap for him, clap for him, yea clap for him

Verse 2- Coach Q

I'm peeping bro just how the game played, you want it all the same day
Then hit the gram until you see that fame fade
My sentiments them filters show you ain't changed,
I'm a product of belief and frequency that's maintained

Song Lyrics

I'm move the needle, I tattooed my campaign

With divisive thoughts bro we not even on the same plane

Aye; somebody tell when where the leaders at

I don't compete, I set um' at tables when they ain't believing yet

I try to see the best; my environment inspires me to stretch

300 push-ups no less discipline in the flesh

I'm tryna teach my people to coalesce; you know more or less

A different route into the Forbes, if you absorb that

Baby steps, read you a book build you a brand

Yea it's options with these stocks' boy you gotta make you a plan

50/50 Feat Robin Raynelle

Intro - Robin Raynelle

They say, two heads are greater than one,

double the back double the front, let's get it done

Independent equals, together lethal

Wanna run it up with you and hit repeat tho

Hook - Coach Q

She wanna know if we going 50/50

I told her stay up off the gram, but I don't think she listening

Listen, who this conversation benefiting

Let's shoot out the city baby, yea we way too busy, Aye

She wanna know if we going 50/50

I told her stay up off the gram, but I don't think she listening

Listen, who this conversation benefiting

Let's shoot out the city baby, yea we way too busy, Aye

Verse 1 – Coach Q

We ain't doing that fraction talking, I don't know what they speaking on

I tell um' actions always come in louder than your speaker phone

They can't compare cause Instagram don't ever see what we been on

It's all division most these podcasters house ain't even home

I know I'm talking slick but you know I'm gone say just what I mean

Song Lyrics

Melo-dating, they about to leave the league without a ring

We stay in our own lane, drive the whip right to the profits

If we going 50-50 it's a 100 band deposit

Lavin all up in the closet, bout to take another flight

Lay you down precise, you know we aint just building for the night

We in the season but it seems like we can focus on the goals

And I know it's going left, soon as you about to scroll.

Verse 2- Robin Raynelle

I tell him meet me in the middle, so much better

Rolling up our sleeves to build thing together

You'll never have to walk this thing along

Reciprocity's philosophy in this home

Coach Q

See everybody want the life that 1% of people live,

They buying all the real estate, we arguing bout paying bills

But we just see so many options, filtered shit ain't even real

The life we want a couple bricks away but we just gotta build

Robin Raynelle

They say, two heads are greater than one,

double the back double the front, let's get it done

Independent equals, together lethal

Wanna run it up with you and hit repeat tho

Coach Q

But see the energy they feeding got us playing enemies

I'm tryna intervene so we can focus on some chemistry

Let's leave the city lease another yacht and dock at Venice beach

And talk about the life we need , what's the team without the queen

Hook - Coach Q

She wanna know if we going 50/50

I told her stay up off the gram, but I don't think she listening

Listen, who this conversation benefiting

Let's shoot out the city baby, yea we way too busy, Aye

She wanna know if we going 50/50

I told her stay up off the gram, but I don't think she listening

Listen, who this conversation benefiting

Let's shoot out the city baby, yea we way too busy, Aye

Girl Dad/MANnerisms

Verse 1- Coach Q

Who am I to be so lucky to have you
A rare jewel that is too precious to value
Girl Dad seems to blush when reminded
But my approach love undermined it
I Had moments where I lost myself
But when I first seen you, I almost lost my breathe
Yeah, you taught me how to love more delicate
Yeah, baby you're my subject and predicate
Passionate intelligent beautiful heaven sent
I'm just praying I ain't too negligent
My momma told me you were gone be my medicine
But when I see you bring me light like Eddison
Interactions help me to grow and evolve
Every single FaceTime it's like you know when to call
If you ever fall I'll be there through it all
I'm just guiding your hand but you're rolling the ball
Watch actions don't match what they saying
Keep your eyes on your feet always know where you stand
Sunraes I've watched you create your demand
Signed Daddy with love… your #1 fan kiss

Switch The Algorithm

Verse 2- Coach Q

What's up young Tez you a prince in my mind

See you following my steps left prints you can find

Mannerisms just like ya pops

Just remember they could never try to fit you in a box

Cydney they always say you remind them of me

Boy we so locked in we ain't ever getting released

Hell even your birthday is even 5 days before mine

Share a special connection is swear it's Devine

Lennox you're my heart you extended my life

You're the reason I fight make sure dreams gone ignite

You the youngest but somehow always give us advice

Conversations at night like you done been here twice

I'm blessed to share love we gone always convene

And love on your moms she is always your Queen

I learned that the season don't ever transpose

Can't eat when it's hot less you plant when it's cold

Value your mind your body your soul

And what you keep in will eventually explode

Don't buy what they sale til you find out the cost,

HoodGeek

Verse 1- Coach Q

It's time to to wake up the culture too much trauma hope it finally change,

All our prodigy's doing 20 years no Bonny James

No Ja morant, well they know how to go live with them hammers up,

So highly influential toxic drama how can they manage us

Aspiring gangsters begging big homies to be a father

Feeling lost but got enough knowledge in them go to Harvard

Told my partners let's build a table build you can catch me where the founders sit

My powers I'm Subconsciously confident and acknowledge it

Listen, I wrote classics in Gotti's basement…

Through my mother and granny's prayers I got passes like I Derrick Mason

Still blood in my fingernails fought my past to amass this greatness

I mediate in different states just to attract to the shit I was chasing

Had conversations with my cousins feel everything been evasive

But the answers in the mirror can't see it until you face it

I walked straight up out the booth now a corporate office adjacent

To ppl that doubt my placement, a genius once you embrace it

Hook

Switch The Algorithm

Aye Embrace Your fam embrace Your teams
Embrace your scars Embrace your future Embrace your dreams
Embrace your past embrace your struggle embrace your demons
Embrace success Embrace what's next Embrace your genius

Verse 2- Coach Q

Aye It's a celebration to break the rules
Things ain't ever quite what it seems so it's always April Fool
HoodGeek the movement it's important to paint pictures,
innovative and creative let's teach them to think quicker
Algorithms that they feed us keep clouding up our perceptions
G had 600 black doctors in Manhattan out buying sections
Now we got black presidents of the National bar association
They Say we wasn't posed to make it,
We ain't just shooting to get on stations
No no no, I don't want no credit, I don't want shine,
I want my ppl to be aligned its too many kids that look like mine,
That's out here dying, all by the design I wish I could tell
them they that they are divine
I wish I could show um or give a sign, wish I had time for brother to find
Out of the womb one of a kind, they using music lock up our minds,
They want us all to get in line I'm sick of um lying we got to keep trying
But let's rewind. …. stay in them books it's time to make it cool,
And calculate your moves always Embrace the things that make you you!

The Goal is the Goal Feat BeHoward and Jodie

Verse 1- BeHoward

I'm making goals like Renaldo and Messi,

Return on your investment is all that you'll be left with,

Life is like dope its bout how far you can stretch it

You want this captain D's well I can teach you how to catch fish, Reel um in

The vision and the discipline is intricate

Everybody did it once it's all about consistency

Man I'm just tryna get fly and go on trips and shit,

Ya missing it, you winning when the interest rates is interesting

Let's get it, If you build it they will come and if its real then they gone run

And that circle that you left with gone kill for what they want

And we aint stopping but the commas on repeat

And we don't need a sidekick its giving Robin was a leach

Rest in peace to negativity, read the room and energy

We want the dividends and synonyms ain't got time for no Diddyin'

Slick shit you can bend but never fold, just remember that the goal is the goal

Verse 2- Coach Q

I don't negotiate, should bet on Pivot if you knew the truth,

I dropped the top on all my plans, yeah, they been through the roof,

Big dreams it ain't ever really what it seems,

Sub conscious intervenes way behind the scenes

Plenty ppl making plenty noise but ain't making plans,

How you on the gram to stance but won't take chance,

I talk about it, orchestrate it, then I implement it

Your last win was 60 seconds, boy it been a minute

Like pulling teeth to get commitment I am not a dentist

I'm living by the Syllable I speak in every sentence

Highly intellectual with discipline is hard to stop,

And I just bought NVidia soon as the market dropped,

Now my proceeds will run you more than some floor seats,

The leader hands down like I'm never playing no D,

I'm out by Sofi and booked the rental for the whole week,

Gotta block excuses like they hit you from a toll free,

Verse 3- Jodie

The goal is the goal I'm about to hit a hat trick

Health, wealth and freedom of time is where I'm at with it

It's specific measurable and achievable

They say its unreachable inconceivable

Song Lyrics

The relevance is heaven sent so it's gotta be time bound

Tenfold my contributions now that's a turnaround

Funny how it come around steam room jacuzzi,

Lifted red ruby's stone cold groovy

Now I'm acting boogie, 750 I ain't tripping

If the interest is hitting, get in line and quickly flip it

Positive hate is silly either dapping or its crickets

Actually, expecting clapping but I'm laughing at these disses

Uncouth egregious, I'm too prestigious

Do whatever to feed us and make it look easy

Not luck just a leader touched by King Jesus

Trust it's set up so our children can precede us

It's a Trend

Hook – Coach Q

Yeah again and again I tell them go do it again

Yeah again and again I do it again and again

Yeah again and again but can you go do it again

Yeah again and again and again I call it a trend

Verse 1 – Coach Q

Yeah I did it again

ain't bragging bout what I done did

I ain't got time to revisit

I said it then that's what it is

I'm watching the climate exposed;

I know what the ppl will say

They keep disposing their chances

they had it then threw it away

I ain't putting diamonds in watches

ain't busting down nothing but doors

When you in love with the process

you don't even look at the score

It's not about money

it's more how to be on the accord

Song Lyrics

When you get yours,

we just gotta make the deposits

our topics is profiting more

They told me to dumb down the Flo

they watching my sequences oh

He said he can't get it in go,

I told um we reap what we sow

They posting that they really want it

but shit never happen before

If you ain't you ain't consistent

then tell me bro how would you know

Verse 2 – Coach Q

Stay on attack like we assembled a pact,

the game is officially Wack

Ppl react without even mentioning facts

I don't intervene I just stack

It's always some noise,

I watch every trap they deploy

I can't even hear by the shores

My momma retiring this year

help my daughter new businesses soar

Told them it's nothing to lose

Switch The Algorithm

interviews so my staff can improve

Every meeting I take on a Friday Soho by the pool

So we just gambling more

on a parlay cause we need a fix;

You acting like you patience don't ever exist

I'm gone keep building it up brick after brick

Designer Habits Feat TheyNeedWeez

Hook- TheyNeedWeez

Got designer habits, expensive fabrics come to fashion she just gotta have it,

Love the attention she attracts that shit automatic,

she already got her caption update her status,

Baby gotta have it

Definitely gone feel the image, even if it's tripping

Cameras on oh they gone see us when we winning

All she know is that we living fast, plus she know that we can get it back

Verse 1 – Coach Q

I told her we don't need no Gucci baby you know I'm more Jeezy,

But if I keep her in exclusive tonight I can call her Fiji

Love designer but it seem like lately I can tell you need it,

Without the latest still they favorite coach so how you gone repeat it,

See it's in you in if it's in you can't go buy it gotta be it

You can try to go go be ASAP but that ain't gone help you Ri it

I seen lines around the mall at Louis V they triple Pd it,

Can't perceive designer money still won't make no one believe it

But see I'm tryna open doors with you just hope you help me key it

Then we watch them bands perform like TSUs, you got to see it

Switch The Algorithm

Watch her switch Dior to Isabel Morant to catch the season

She don't ever need a reason status read we leaving Neiman's

Hook- TheyNeedWeez

Got designer habits, expensive fabrics come to fashion she just gotta have it,

Love the attention she attracts that shit automatic,

she already got her caption update her status,

Baby gotta have it

Definitely gone feel the image, even if it's tripping

Cameras on oh they gone see us when we winning

All she know is that we living fast, plus she know that we can get it back

Verse 2- Coach Q

Yeah we wake up check the market early them our Main adventures,

Plus we catch attention when we coming out like Damon's dentures

People posting pictures when their lives just don't match the description

Taylor made decisions Amiri linen be shit be consistent,

But see they selling dreams, facades and schemes

But tell me who is supplying the means

Do anything we buy the steams, we filling voids, we making me memes

But long as I keep wifey clean, she loves that we don't price thing

But she knows when it's time to stack the movie done, we off the scene

We always had the spending power never catch the synergy

Song Lyrics

It's like we ain't had coffee we can't ever keep that energy

But soon as we know them cameras rolling everything is cinematic

Blinded by the status see we all got them designs habits

Bring the Love back

Verse 1 – Coach Q

Who am I to judge you for navigating what you have been through,

Lead with emotions just to go can take it back like a rental

We put love on intermission and we torn hyper extensions

No surgeon can come and fix it we patch it up with attention

Was driving my son to school talking adjectives and division

He mentioned this girl in class had a crush hell i started grinning

Extended moments of innocence teaching him to deserve it

Cause karma hand out the sentences never read you a verdict

Still tryna advise him while moisture exits my eyelids

I know my life has comprised of these years without compromising,

I'm kinda sick of disguising so many moving like islands

Isolation is tiring when love is all you desiring

Verse 2- Coach Q

Now we Fean for compassion I'm asking cause I need something too,

It's like we dating and thrifting I look around and I don't see nothing new

It's the energy given not how you view your condition

so many seeking admission but never paying tuition

Baby let's get back to the loving disarming seem like we been at war,

Your eyes tell me the story you leaving out you need something more

Song Lyrics

Noticed we on the same page number just reading different books

They say the worst chance you can take is the one that's never took,

I'm just bringing love, love myself love my mom,

Love my kids enough to challenge every habit I been on,

Love my pops, love my fam love the lessons from mistakes,

Destination focused but loving the process that it takes

Acknowledgements

First and foremost, I want to thank God for giving me an opportunity to share my gifts with the world.

I want to express my deepest gratitude to my mother, Tonya McDaniel, who has been my guiding light since the day I was born. My father, Willard Clark, thank you for showing me from a very young age that excellence was possible. My Grandmother Alma Clark and Stepdad Kenneth Mcdaniel

My four amazing children Cyntez, Cydney, Raegan, and Caiden. Every day you have been the driving force behind everything I do.

My closest friends Eddie Stevenson, Jodie Smith, and Robert Washington. You've been there with me through every high and low. Ashley Clark, your influence has been instrumental in my journey.

My sister Tonisha Gordon and Brother Dionte White. My entire family of Aunts, Uncles, and cousins. Joshua Mundy, my business partner who became like a brother!

Countless other friends, business partners, mentors, and individuals who have inspired, guided, and supported me throughout this journey. Thank you for being a part of my story.

About the Author

Quawn Clark is a devoted father of four children: Cyntez, Cydney, Raegan, and Caiden. Quawn's love for his children has been the guiding force behind his personal and professional journey. From a young age, Quawn has been driven by a desire to inspire others, always knowing that his calling in life is to help people unlock their full potential and become the best versions of themselves. His path has been one of constant evolution, from his early years as a rapper, to becoming a tech enthusiast, and ultimately transforming into a purpose-driven entrepreneur.

As the co-founder of Pivot Tech School, Quawn has been instrumental in creating opportunities for individuals from underrepresented backgrounds to break into the tech industry. With a focus on diversity and inclusion, Pivot Tech has empowered people of all races, genders, and experiences to gain the skills and confidence they need to succeed in the fast-paced world of technology. For Quawn, building Pivot Tech wasn't just about teaching tech but creating a movement that would break down barriers and open doors for those who may have otherwise been overlooked.

Quawn is also the founder of HoodGeek, an initiative that reflects his deep commitment to changing the narrative around intelligence and success for people from inner-city communities. HoodGeek is about more than just promoting education; it's about showing the world that brilliance, creativity, and ambition can thrive no matter where you come from. Quawn's unique perspective and ability to bridge the gap between street smarts and academic intelligence have made him a trusted voice in both tech and culture.

Known to many as "Coach Q," Quawn's passion for mentorship and personal development shines through in everything he does. Whether he's coaching aspiring entrepreneurs, speaking to young professionals, or guiding his own children through life's challenges, Quawn brings a sense of purpose, integrity, and inspiration to every interaction. He firmly believes that genuine relationships are the foundation of a meaningful life, and he strives to build those connections in all areas of his work.

Outside of his professional endeavors, Quawn enjoys basketball, traveling, working out, and turning innovative ideas into real-world success. He's a firm believer that each of us has been blessed with a genius-level ability—a unique gift from God that we must learn to recognize, nurture, and embrace. Whether through his writing, speaking, or coaching, Quawn is on a mission to inspire others to discover their own genius and live a life of purpose and fulfillment.

As a leader, mentor, and father, Quawn's ultimate goal is to leave a lasting impact on the world by uplifting others and creating spaces where people can thrive, grow, and succeed on their own terms.

Picture Credits

#1 Josh Mundy & Quawn Clark

#2 Quawn Clark

#3 Orlando Pender & Jodie Smith

#4 Robert Washington & Jodie Smith

#5 Cydney Shaw & Cyntez Shaw

#6 Tonya McDaniel, Tonisha Gordan, & Quawn Clark

Yourcoachq

Quawn Clark

Quawn Clark–Pivot Tech Solutions, LLC

www.yourcoachq.com